Toronto Sketches 4

"The Way We Were"

Toronto Sketches 4

"The Way We Were"

Mike Filey

DUNDURN PRESS
Toronto & Oxford

Edited by Nadine Stoikoff
Printed and bound in Canada by Webcom

The publisher wishes to acknowledge the generous assistance and ongoing support of the **Canada Council**, the **Book Publishing Industry Development Program** of the **Department of Canadian Heritage**, the **Ontario Arts Council**, the **Ontario Publishing Centre** of the **Ministry of Citizenship, Culture and Recreation,** and the **Ontario Heritage Foundation.**
     Care has been taken to trace the ownership of copyright material used in the text (including the illustrations). The author and publisher welcome any information enabling them to rectify any reference or credit in subsequent editions.

J. Kirk Howard, Publisher

Canadian Cataloguing in Publication Data

Filey, Mike, 1941–
     Toronto sketches 4 : "the way we were"

ISBN 1-55002-248-2

1. Toronto (Ont.) – History.   I. Title.

FC3097.4.F55 1995   971.3'541   C95-932542-5
F1059.5.T6857F55 1995

Dundurn Press Limited
2181 Queen Street East
Suite 301
Toronto, Canada
M4E 1E5

Dundurn Distribution
73 Lime Walk
Headington, Oxford
England
0X3 7AD

Dundurn Press Limited
1823 Maryland Avenue
P.O. Box 1000
Niagara Falls, N.Y.
U.S.A. 14302-1000

CONTENTS

Note: Date indicates the edition of the Toronto *Sunday Sun* in which the column originally appeared.

PREFACE

During what were to be the last few months of its life, the late, lamented *Toronto Telegram* would occasionally feature a few of my old Toronto photographs on the last page of the Saturday paper's real estate section. I say occasionally because the chance of my material getting into print any particular Saturday really depended on whether they were able to sell all the section pages to advertisers. If they could, I was out; if they couldn't, I was in. Hopefully, the presence of my material or, conversely, the non-appearance of my stuff had little to do with the good old *Tely*'s demise on Saturday, October 30, 1971, exactly ninety-five years and 195 days after Volume 1, Number 1, of what owner John Ross Robertson had originally called *The Evening Telegram* first appeared.

On November 1, 1971, the *Toronto Sun* was born with its publisher, Doug Creighton, and many of his editors and reporters still reeling from the *Telegram*'s untimely death just two days before, and now eager to ensure the success of their new responsibility that many nay-sayers believed would be just as dead as the *Tely* before very many issues had been published. How wrong they were.

My connection with the early editions of the *Sun* continued to be on a once-in-a-while basis and it wasn't until the Sunday edition had become a success that my "The Way We Were" column began to appear with any regularity. Now that I think about it, it was twenty years ago, 1975, that the column became a consistent component of the *Sunday Sun*. And in that twenty-year period, I've only missed one column, and it wasn't even my fault. It was the Sunday they over-sold advertising space and I was dumped for a Crisco ad.

The previously published trio of Toronto sketches, *Toronto Sketches*, *More Toronto Sketches*, and *Toronto Sketches 3* (now the selection of the title for the new book becomes a little more obvious, right?), covered a somewhat random sampling of those 1,299 columns (it would have been an even 1,300 but for the Crisco ad). *Toronto Sketches 4* contains my *Sunday Sun* columns that appeared in the paper during the period August 7, 1994, to

July 30, 1995. As one can appreciate, the very nature of my columns frequently prompts readers to respond (especially if I've spelled a relative's name incorrectly or if a locomotive's wheel arrangement is mistakenly altered). If the original column generated interesting feedback, that material has been included in a box following the pertinent column. I've also included any details received as a result of the appearance of the column in the belief that they, too, will enhance the original story. Should you, dear reader, wish to add your two-cents worth please do so addressing your comments to me, c/o the publisher, whose address appears on page iv.

Unless otherwise indicated, all photographs are taken from my private collection.

Mike Filey
Willowdale, Ontario

ACKNOWLEDGEMENTS

A s well as being a welcome source of money (after all, somebody has to pay for the film, a few blank computer discs, and an occasional trip to the Beach, the nice one out Queen Street East where the faithful Dundurn Press staff toil and not those hot, sandy ones in Florida), my *Sun* column has put me in touch with a lot of nice people over the years. Most important, of course, are the faithful readers, many of whom have supplied me with interesting column material (or corrections). Then there's the *Sun* library staff (Julie, Cathy, Joyce, Glenna, Sue, and Catherine) who may make rude noises when I tell a great joke, but are nevertheless totally professional when I ask for their assistance. And there's Vena and Marilyn who make sure my material is always in their computer on time, and Ed and Dave who make sure that same material looks good when it comes out and hits the page. My thanks also to Irene and the staff at the Charles Abel photo lab and to Douglas who builds and talks to computers.

A special thanks to the people at Dundurn Press, especially Kirk, Nadine, and Andy, and to the various archives (TTC, City of Toronto, Toronto Harbour Commission, and Metro Toronto Public Library) and their archivists who have always responded positively when I've requested the use of an old photograph from their respective collections.

And most of all, thanks to my wife, Yarmila, who, in addition to just being there for the past twenty-seven years, was also the person to put me in touch with Wordperfect.

for Yarmila

A LITTLE BIT OF T.O.
August 7, 1994

*A little bit of "this" and a little bit of "that" for this week's
"The Way We Were" column.*

THIS NO. 1

A couple of new books on totally different aspects of our city's history have recently come to my attention. The first documents in word and photo the long and fascinating history of Havergal College, its Avenue Road campus (on the east side, just south of Lawrence) long a familiar North Toronto landmark.

The new evangelical school for girls, as Havergal was described in 1894, the year of its birth, was the brainchild of a group of prominent local religious leaders and businessmen (many of whom had helped create Ridley College in St. Catharines five years before). To house their new Havergal College (the name was selected to honour Frances Ridley Havergal, prominent English poet and hymn writer), the founders rented an old residence at 350 Jarvis Street. The house may have been old, but at least it was on the most fashionable street in the young city of 175,000 inhabitants.

The founders also agreed to jointly cover any deficits incurred during the school's first year and to appoint Miss Ellen Knox, a teacher on staff at Cheltenham Ladies' College in England, as the school's first principal.

This statue of John Graves Simcoe (now sans sword), standing at Queen's Park, is one of many statues scattered throughout Toronto.

Miss Knox was there to welcome the first students when the new school's doors opened for the first time on September 11, 1894.

One hundred years have gone by and much has happened. To capture the Havergal story former student Mary Byers has written *Havergal, Celebrating a Century*, a memory-filled hardcover book which is available for thirty-eight dollars at the school or forty-two dollars by mail from Havergal College Centennial Office, 1451 Avenue Road, Toronto, Ontario M4N 2H9. For more information call (416) 480-6520.

The second book though less weighty and therefore less expensive is, in its own way, just as fascinating. *Sculpture/Toronto* by June Ardiel (Leidra Books) is the perfect reference book for those of us who, while touring our great city, frequently come upon pieces of sculptured art work and wonder (usually out loud) "what the heck is that?"

In June's book, nearly 300 free-standing historical and contemporary sculptures on view in public spaces throughout Metro and created by no less than 178 different artists from all over the world (*Angel of Peace* by Charles Keck, south of the Bandshell at the CNE, *The Archer* by Henry Moore, on Nathan Phillips Square, *Meet* by Kosso Eloul, at 1111 Finch Avenue West, and more) are identified and described.

THIS NO. 2

This year the various gates to the good old Canadian National Exhibition will swing open on Friday, August 19 (this year it's an eighteen-day event, cut back from the usual twenty days, with a Friday rather than a Wednesday opening). In another departure from the norm, the traditional opening ceremonies will take place on the evening (usually its an afternoon event) of the eighteenth at the Bandshell. A tradition that does remain, however, is the selection of a person of prominence to actually open the fair. This year rather than 'a' person it'll be a 'bunch' of persons in the form of the Toronto Mendelssohn Choir. This world-famous organization is celebrating its centennial this year, having been established in 1894 by Augustus Stephen Vogt. The choir will perform a forty-five-minute 'mini-concert' as part of the opening ceremonies.

THIS NO. 3

While on the subject of local musical groups, my recent column on the Four Lads prompted a note from Bernard O'Grady advising that the alumni of St. Michael's Choir School, the *Lads'* alma mater (and the alma mater of hundreds of other grads including Michael "Phantom" Burgess and John "Danny Boy" McDermott) are seeking other graduates for a planned reunion. Want more details? Drop Bernard a line at St. Michael's Choir School, 13 Victoria Street West, Alliston, Ontario L9R 1S9.

Havergal College was the most fashionable place on the block at its official opening in May 1927.

THAT NO. 1

If you're travelling in the Almonte area of the province west of Ottawa on Highway 44, be sure to drop by the recently opened Naismith Visitors Centre. "Who was Naismith," you ask? Shame. He's the Canadian(!!) who gave the world the game of basketball. Dr. James Naismith was born in 1861 on a farm north of the town and educated in the local school system before moving on to McGill University in Montreal where he eventually became athletic director. In 1891 Naismith joined the staff of the YMCA Training School in Springfield, Massachusetts, where he developed an indoor game suitable for winter play. Using a ball and peach baskets into which the ball was thrown, it was only natural Naismith's new game be called basketball. For more information, call (613) 256-1976.

Since this column appeared Canadian-born James Naismith's game of basketball has come 'home' with two Canadian cities about to enter the National Basketball Association. Vancouver will have its Grizzlies; Toronto, its Raptors. The Toronto entry will play its first two seasons at SkyDome before moving to the remodelled City Postal Delivery Building at Bay Street and Lake Shore Boulevard in the fall of 1997. See the January 15, 1995 column.

SHUFFLE OFF TO BUFFALO
August 14, 1994

T his week's column comes complete with an apology to the folks in the Travel Department. However, I figure if they can travel thither and yon to research stories, so, too, can I, though my thither and yon are a little closer to home; Buffalo and Rochester, to be precise.

• • •

The marble memorial to John Blocher, shoe innovator.

It's funny how times change. When I was a teenager, a trip to Buffalo, New York, was an eagerly anticipated event for whatever reason; shopping, dining, imbibing, etc. But as Toronto grew into a so-called 'world-class' city (boy I hate that description), we suddenly began to look down our noses at the American city at the end of the Queen Elizabeth Way.

However, after our recent and all-too-brief stay, I'm here to tell you that Buffalo is still an interesting place to visit with all kinds of history peering from its weary old downtown buildings, with dozens of architectural gems strung out like pearls along Delaware Avenue and lots of fascinating places to explore; the most fascinating, in my estimation, being the city's incredibly beautiful Forest Lawn Cemetery.

In the beginning Buffalo, like Toronto, was a rather insignificant settlement in the wilderness. In fact, both communities can trace their origins to the arrival of their respective first white settlers in the last years of the 1700s. Several decades later, each community suffered badly as a result of enemy raids during the War of 1812.

Just as the origin of the name Toronto is uncertain ("a place of meeting" is the accepted translation from the Mississauga language, but there are a host of other possibilities), so, too, is the exact origin of the term Buffalo. Some say it's from Buffaloe, the name of a person of

Trolley tours Buffalo style.

mixed parentage who, having been rejected by his tribe because of white man's blood flowing through his veins, came east to seek solace, eventually making camp on the bank of a small watercourse that flowed into the Niagara River. In time that watercourse became known as Buffaloe's Creek and it wasn't long before the nearby community took the abbreviated version, Buffalo, as its name.

Or was it named for the misidentified buffalo bones unearthed near the townsite? All we really know is that the original name of the community, New Amsterdam, selected to honour the pioneer Dutch land speculators who purchased hundreds of thousands of acres of lands in western New York State from the native people, didn't last long at all.

Buffalo's boom period started with the decision to make it the site of the western terminus of the Erie Canal. On October 26, 1825, Lake Erie was connected with the Hudson River via 'Clinton's Ditch.' Buffalo's future never looked brighter.

• • •

To make sure you get the most out of your visit, take the two-hour tour on a replica old-fashioned trolley and hope your driver is Vic, whose commentary isn't limited just to stories about the outside of old buildings but includes some of the juicier inside stories at City Hall as well. Seats on the trolley should be reserved by calling Trolley Tours of Buffalo at (716) 885-8825 in advance.

A few facts unleashed by Vic during our drive through Buffalo: Pilot Field, named for the Pilot Trucking Company who put up a lot of money to build the 19,500-seat sports stadium in the heart of the city, offers two sizes of ice-cubes for drinks; a small version for those sitting under cover, a larger size for those sitting in the sun. The U.S. Navy destroyer *The Sullivans* moored in the six-acre Naval & Servicemen's Park on the beautifully rejuvenated Buffalo waterfront honours the five Sullivan brothers who died while serving on the same ship during the Second World War. (As a result of this tragedy, then President Roosevelt passed a law that no more than two members of the same family could serve on the same ship.) There are no less than five Frank Lloyd Wright-designed houses in Buffalo, two of them not far from a pair of houses selected from the Sears & Roebuck catalogue. Buffalo was home to a pair of U.S. presidents, Millard Fillmore and Grover Cleveland, the latter also serving as mayor of Buffalo, the former one of 147,000 souls interred in Forest Lawn Cemetery which is also on the tour. In fact the trolley drives right through the grounds, much to the delight

Tall and proud, Buffalo's City Hall, which opened in 1930, is an excellent example of art-deco architecture.

of the cemetery management who take great pride in their immaculately cared for property. Other 'residents' include John McVean, a Canadian who received the Medal of Honor during the American Civil War, Willis Carrier, the father of the air-conditioning industry, William Fargo of Wells Fargo Express, and John Blocher, creator of the left and right shoe (previously all

shoes were the same shape). The extraordinary Blocher monument, with its four life-size figures in white marble posed in a sort of sculptured diorama behind one-inch-thick glass walls, is a 'must see' in the cemetery.

In a couple of weeks we'll travel the New York Thruway to Rochester, a city that also has a lot to offer the day-tripper.

Downtown Buffalo.

DOWN AT THE GOOD OL' EX
August 21, 1994

There are few things you can completely rely on in this day and age. Two of the certainties are the monthly telephone bill and the arrival each August of the grand old lady of the waterfront (no sexism or disrespect intended), the Canadian National Exhibition. It must be difficult for newcomers to our community to understand the impact the Ex had on those of us who were fortunate enough to grow up in this great city.

The Ex was where we went to see the next year's De Soto, Packard, Studebaker, in fact all the new cars first. It was where companies like Halicrafters, Sylvania, and Admiral introduced us to those wooden boxes with little glass screens on which funny flickering black and white pictures actually moved around. Would this thing called television really last? And which rooftop aerial was the best, and was a rotor really necessary?

The Ex introduced me to something called stereophonic sound, one giant step up from hi-fi (for high-fidelity). That was back in the days when you could go into a store and buy a needle and no one would think anything of it. After all, a worn needle played havoc with the grooves on your LP records. (I can hear it now, "What does LP stand for? What's a record?")

As a teenager it was my good fortune to get summer employment with a company called Fleetwood, and every day of the CNE I'd demonstrate the effects of stereo sound by playing those 'ping-pong' demonstration records. Visitors by the hundreds would stop by the booth in the old Electrical Building and stare at the speakers, moving their heads from side to side as the little ball bounced back and forth between the woofers and tweeters. Every once in a while I'd give them a real thrill and put on one of those jet flypast sound-effect platters. (Remember when records were called platters?)

Each year, without fail, the Ex would introduce us to things new and marvelous. Today most of those discoveries have become as commonplace as the hand-held two-dollar numerical calculator, the ancestors of which were introduced to the public in the old Business Machines Building at the west end of the CNE grounds where the geodesic domes stand today.

One of the most popular features of the annual fair will celebrate its fortieth anniversary this year on August 24. Erected in 1954, the Food Building (known officially as the Food Products Building) was the first new building (not counting the 1948 Grandstand or 1931 Bandshell) to be erected on the CNE grounds since the magnificent new Horse Palace opened twenty-three years earlier.

The present Food Building replaced the Ex's first Food Building (officially, the Pure Food Building and for a time the Pure Food and International Building) that opened in time for the 1922 edition of the CNE. Though much smaller than today's sprawling building, it was on the same site.

• • •

The year 1954 was special for the Ex for another reason. It was in that year that a sixteen-year-old Toronto schoolgirl surprised everyone by becoming the first person to conquer the frigid and treacherous waters of Lake Ontario. Marilyn Bell's heroic twenty-hour, fifty-six-minute crossing from the United States Coast Guard station at Wilson, New York, to the breakwater in front of the Boulevard Club on September 8 and 9 remains as one of the country's all-time great sporting accomplishments and arguably, perhaps (with the Blue Jays World Series triumphs), the most spectacular and dramatic event in Toronto's two-hundred-year history.

Marathon swims at the annual fair had been introduced in 1927, and while it was expected that Toronto's George Young, who had unexpectedly won the Wrigley Swim in California the previous year, would be the first to complete the twenty-one-mile triangular course off the CNE waterfront, it was not to be. The youngster was defeated by German Ernst Vierkoetter, an outcome that was highly unpopular in the very British Toronto of the day.

This type of marathon continued on and off over the next few years. Then in early 1954, CNE officials announced that they had contracted with long-distance swimmer Florence Chadwick to swim across Lake Ontario. If Florence was successful she would be paid $10,000; if she failed, the American swimmer would get nothing.

This obvious rejection of Canadian swimmers by CNE officials upset many people including Marilyn and her coach, Gus Ryder. Nevertheless, the sixteen-year-old would try the crossing anyway.

Entering the water just minutes after the more experienced Florence, Marilyn soon overtook the American and took aim on the CNE grounds more than thirty miles in the murky distance.

Nearly twenty-one hours after she entered the bone-chilling water, a weary Marilyn touched the breakwater south of the Boulevard Club to become the first person to swim Lake Ontario. The entire country went wild. Oh, by the way, the CNE did come through with the $10,000 prize money. And it would be tax free, Ottawa decreed.

The following year Marilyn swam the English Channel, and in 1956 the Strait of Juan de Fuca.

Marilyn Bell, the original "Sweetheart of the Lake," signs the guest book at City Hall after her ticker-tape parade up Bay Street in honour of her historic swim of Lake Ontario in 1954.

REMEMBERING THE *EMPRESS*
August 28, 1994

On several occasions I have commented in this column on how unfortunate it is that Canadian school children are taught copious quantities of world history while being subjected to very little about the history of their own country. A case in point. Ask any student what the British-registered, American-owned *Titanic* was and undoubtedly they will be aware of that ill-starred vessel's sad ending in the North Atlantic that cold night in April 1912.

The ill-fated *Empress of Ireland* that sank in the St. Lawrence River exactly eighty years ago with the loss of 1,012 souls. Of this number 840 were passengers. A total of 832 passengers went down on *Titanic* two years earlier.

Now ask that same student about the Canadian Pacific liner *Empress of Ireland* and chances are you'll draw a blank, even though the total number of passengers who died in the *Empress* disaster following the steamship's sinking in the St. Lawrence River near Rimouski, Quebec, eighty years ago, May 29, 1914, exceeded the number of passengers who drowned in the *Titanic* tragedy two years before.

I hope I've piqued your curiosity about this event in Canadian history and if I have you can learn more about the *Empress of Ireland* and see some of the artifacts recovered from the wreck in the Salvation Army display in Centennial Square at this year's CNE. What's the 'Sally Ann's' connection with the disaster, you ask? As anyone who has accompanied me on my walks through Mt. Pleasant Cemetery and gazed upon the Army's *Empress of Ireland* memorial will know, the Salvation Army lost more than 150 of its ranks including all but nine of the thirty-nine-member Canadian Staff Band. The majority of the Army's victims were from Toronto.

• • •

The Hospital for Incurables, Dunn Avenue, Parkdale, circa 1900. This building was replaced in 1979 by the present modern structure. The hospital's other facility is on University Avenue just north of Elm Street.

This year marks the 120th anniversary of the opening of what is today known far and wide as the Queen Elizabeth Hospital, though when the institution first opened on May 6, 1874, the sign over the door at its original Bathurst and King street location displayed the rather repulsive title, Toronto Home for Incurables. The 'Home' had been established to lessen the burden that long-term care patients, those with untreatable forms of consumption (TB), heart disease, and paralysis, were imposing on the city's main hospital, the Toronto General, then located on Gerrard Street East just west of the Don.

As serious as this problem was, the lack of accommodation for the seriously afflicted who lacked the monetary means to seek what little medical treatment that was available then was another reason for the Home's existence. Without it these unfortunates would continue to be incarcerated, virtually without hope, in the local House of Industry.

To help alleviate the situation, several community-minded citizens, led by Mayor Alexander Manning (Manning Avenue), banded together and established the first Home for Incurables in the early spring of 1894, moving the institution into larger premises on Dunn Avenue in suburban Parkdale five years later, and continued to expand several times over the next few years.

Then in 1941, the first of several name changes occurred; first to the Queen Elizabeth (in honour of the present Queen Mother) Hospital for Incurables; twenty years later it became, simply, the Queen Elizabeth

Hospital. In 1975 the Queen Elizabeth affiliated with the University of Toronto to become the first chronic care/teaching hospital in the country.

Over the next few years, as the population continued to age followed by increasing demands for chronic- and long-term care facilities, the hospital expanded dramatically. The former Mt. Sinai Hospital on University Avenue was acquired (a new Mt. Sinai opened further up the avenue) followed in 1979 by the development of a progressive new facility on the old Dunn Avenue site.

Since its opening more than 120 years ago, the Queen Elizabeth Hospital has grown and evolved into a 601-bed specialized chronic

The unusual Thomas Foster Memorial, five and a half kilometres north of Uxbridge, Ontario, will be open to visitors this coming September 4 and 18, 1994.

care and rehabilitation centre. Donations to help the hospital prepare for its next 120 years would be gratefully received by the Queen Elizabeth Hospital Foundation, 550 University Avenue, Toronto, Ontario M5G 2A2.

• • •

Many columns ago I wrote about the Thomas Foster Memorial, a most unique and unusual structure erected in 1935–36 by the former Toronto mayor as a tribute to his late wife and to his only daughter, who had died in only her eleventh year. The Byzantine-style temple, described as the most lavish on the continent in a contemporary newspaper article, sits on a hill just north of the community of Uxbridge. Since my article appeared, the time-weary structure has become the responsibility of the Township of Uxbridge and great strides have been made to prevent the memorial's further deterioration. The public will have an opportunity to explore the mausoleum (Foster, too, was buried within the Memorial following his death in 1945) from 1:00 PM to 5:00 PM on September 4 and again on September 18, 1994. Call Barbara Pratt at Blue Heron Books in Uxbridge at (905) 852-4282) for more details.

TINY CABIN'S THE OLDEST
September 4, 1994

One of the most frequently asked questions when it comes to 'Toronto trivia' (mmm ... wonder if there's a board game there somewhere) is where does one find the *oldest* building in the city.

Many believe that the structures within the ramparts of historic Fort York are the oldest. Not so. While it is true that Lieutenant-Governor Simcoe's fort was established in 1793 to provide protection against an anticipated invasion from south of the border, most of the original buildings suffered severe damage during the American invasion of 1813 and were replaced, while others simply deteriorated to the point where they had to be pulled down before they fell down.

That's not to say the structures at the fort aren't ancient (several blockhouses date from 1813), it's just that they're not the oldest in Toronto. (The whole story about Fort York can be found in Carl Benn's fascinating book *Historic Fort York 1793–1993*, published by Natural Heritage/Natural History Inc.)

Actually, the honour of being the oldest structure in town belongs to the tiny Scadding Cabin located a short distance northwest of the CNE Bandshell in Exhibition Place. In fact, this year marks the cabin's 200th anniversary, so if you're going to the Ex today or tomorrow why not stop by

The little Scadding Cabin can be seen in this early view of the Ex's first permanent building, the magnificent Crystal Palace. Though the cabin remains in this same location today (see arrow), note the Lake Ontario shoreline (now the site of the Lake Shore Boulevard, south of the Ex) and (bottom left) the long-gone Dufferin Street wharf where 'commuter' boats from the city disembarked their happy passengers.

Some of the York Pioneers on their way to the Exhibition grounds to assist in the rebuilding of the historic Scadding Cabin, August 22, 1879.

and wish the old building and the York Pioneers, who look after the cabin, a 'happy birthday.'

Unlike the old buildings at Fort York (and perhaps this is where the fort's blockhouses could take the honour if the question was modified to read "the oldest building still in its original location"), the Scadding Cabin was built in 1794 on the east bank of the Don River just south of the dusty road leading easterly out of the tiny community towards Kingston, a thoroughfare known back then, naturally enough, as the Kingston Road and now as Queen Street.

• • •

The owner of what was to become known as the Scadding Cabin was one John Scadding who was born in Devonshire, England, in 1754. While little is known of his early life, research does reveal that Scadding was hired as manager of a large estate at nearby Wolford owned by Ontario's future first lieutenant-governor.

Scadding didn't just work for John Simcoe, he was also one of his most trusted friends. Therefore, it was only natural that when, in 1791, the British government selected Simcoe to establish and govern a new province in British North America, a province we now know as Ontario, he would ask his loyal employee and friend to join him.

Scadding arrived in Upper Canada, as the new province was first called, in 1792 and assumed his duties as Simcoe's clerk. When sickness forced the lieutenant-governor to return to England in 1796, Scadding accompanied him, returning to his duties as manager of the vast estate at Wolford.

A dozen years after Simcoe's death in 1806, Scadding rounded up the members of his family, wife, Melicent, and sons John, Jr., Charles, and Henry, and returned to Upper Canada settling on land he had been granted by the Crown during his first visit to the new province.

His grant was described, officially, as Lot 15, Concession 1, Broken Front, and consisted of 253 acres bordered by the then winding Don River on the west and the original lake shore to the south, and today's Broadview Avenue and Danforth Avenue to the east and north, respectively.

It was on this property that Scadding had erected a log house soon after his arrival in 1792. Unfortunately, in the depth of the winter of 1794, that house burned to the ground and a second house was quickly built to replace it. The site of this new residence would today be in the middle of the Don Valley Parkway just south of the Queen Street bridge.

The Scadding Cabin today.

Soon after his return to York (Toronto) in 1818, Scadding sold his property (which included the old cabin) to William Smith whose son, John, eventually offered the relic to the newly established York Pioneers and Historical Society.

This organization (which still meets regularly to talk over various facets of Toronto's rich history) arranged with the officials of the equally new Toronto Industrial Exhibition (after 1904, Canadian National Exhibition) to have the Scadding Cabin moved, log by log, from its original site and re-erected on the Exhibition grounds in time for the opening on September 5, 1879, of the first Exhibition. It's been an attraction at the Ex ever since.

• • •

I need some help. A reader wonders when a 747, transporting a NASA shuttle piggy-back, flew over Toronto? Was it in the late seventies or early eighties? I saw it, but forgot the actual date. Any ideas? If you do, please drop me a note.

The answer appeared at the end of my September 25, 1994 column.

COMIN' ROUND
September 11, 1994

May 16, 1853, dawned bright, sunny, and warm, and all along Front Street curious Torontonians (of whom there were approximately 35,000 according to the most reliable records) gathered in eager anticipation to witness the inaugural run of the young province's first steam locomotive.

Engine number 2 of the newly franchised Ontario, Simcoe, and Huron Railway, so-named as they were the three lakes to be served by this pioneer transport company, was proudly christened *Toronto* and was the twenty-four-ton creation of the craftsmen at John Good's rambling foundry situated on the north side of Queen Street between Yonge and Victoria, well to the north and west of the busy city's dynamic downtown business district around King and Church streets.

As the scheduled departure time approached, several proud railway hands backed the shiny new engine and tender out of the wooden shed erected near the Front and Bay street corner and in which the engine and tender had been housed since their arrival from the foundry, a delicate moving procedure that involved sections of temporary track, pinch bars, and the strength of numerous sweaty laborers.

The crew then proceeded to couple the engine and tender to a boxcar and a passenger car, the fire was stoked with wood, appropriate words were

The John Street Roundhouse (under construction) and the Toronto skyline, 1929. Note Royal York Hotel (see arrow) in both photos accompanying this column.

offered by the assembled dignitaries, and off chugged the historic train, consisting of two cars, first going west along the city's waterfront, then northward for Machell's Corners (to be renamed the following year Aurora), reaching, as the contemporary newspapers reported, a maximum speed of 15 MPH. The railway age had finally arrived here in the Province of Ontario (or more correctly, the Province of Upper Canada; the name change not taking place until another fourteen years had passed and confederation achieved).

Though it was but a minor element in the fascinating story of Ontario's first railway, that small wooden shed near the Front and Bay corner was to be the forerunner of a multitude of ancillary railway structures scattered across the city's constantly changing waterfront that over the following decades were to be erected, remodelled, demolished, and, in the case of the John Street roundhouse, rehabilitated. This latter action will take place in conjunction with the proposed expansion of the Metro Toronto Convention Centre.

Built by the Canadian Pacific Railway in 1929–32, the John Street roundhouse replaced a similar, but smaller, fifteen-bay structure that had been erected in 1897 to serve the hundreds of coal-fired locomotives that hauled the all-vital inter-city passenger and freight trains of the era.

As evidenced by the ever-increasing size of steam locomotives, the replacement roundhouse was designed as a forty-eight-bay structure, though only thirty-two stalls were constructed. Many of these bays were built with a 130-foot length to accommodate the huge new steam engines being built to haul the ever-lengthening freight trains serving the furthest reaches of the fast-growing country. The integral three-point turntable is 120 feet in length and was designed to permit engines to be rotated after servicing, eliminating expensive 'run around' track.

The John Street structure was the first in Canada to include a provision for 'direct steaming' that permitted locomotives to be run into and out of the roundhouse using steam generated off-site. This cut down significantly on the smoke pollution problem inherent with most steam locomotive servicing facilities and permitted faster turn-around times.

Abandoned by the CPR in the mid-1980s, the John Street facility remains today as one of the few surviving roundhouses that were once so familiar across this vast land. You can help decide its future.

• • •

The province of Ontario has set up a Task Force, under the auspices of the Hon. David Crombie of the Waterfront Regeneration Trust, to investigate the concept of converting the former CPR John Street Roundhouse into an operating rail heritage museum. The Task Force's mandate is to develop a

Similar view, 1994. The roundhouse awaits its rejuvenation.

program and conceptual plan for this museum, a concept plan for the new park (known as either Roundhouse or Central Park) that will be created around the historic structure, and a feasibility and business plan for the construction and on-going day-to-day operation of the museum.

To assist the Task Force with its assignment, any member of the public or group wishing to contribute views or information on any aspect of the mandate is invited to meet, informally, with the Task Force on Wednesday, September 14, 1994, at the offices of the Trust. If interested, please call (416) 314-9490 to arrange for a specific time. Written submissions are also welcome and should be addressed to the Task Force, c/o Waterfront Regeneration Trust, 207 Queen's Quay West, Suite 580, Toronto M5J 1A7.

• • •

Solo Swims of Ontario will be sponsoring the unveiling of a special commemorative plaque at Niagara-on-the-Lake (Gazebo Park, foot of King Street) on Saturday, October 29, 1994, in honour of the more than thirty athletes who have crossed Lake Ontario since the historic first crossing by Toronto schoolgirl Marilyn Bell exactly forty years ago. Many of the athletes are expected to attend the event and the public is cordially invited.

With work now well under way on the $180-million expansion of the Metro Toronto Convention Centre, bays 1–11 of the historic CPR roundhouse have been dismantled with the stored bricks ready to be reassembled when construction of underground exhibit areas and ballroom have been completed. While future uses of the roundhouse have yet to be determined, development of the adjacent fifteen-acre Roundhouse Park is well under way.

GREAT ENTERTAINMENT
September 18, 1994

As disappointing as the early end to this year's baseball season is, something positive has come out of the whole sorry mess. With visitors arriving in town with prepaid hotel reservations, they are now free to see another part of Toronto, our lively theatre scene. As a result, the big-ticket shows, *Show Boat, Phantom of the Opera, Miss Saigon,* and others, are playing to packed houses in their respective incredibly lavish playhouses. There's one other show that's doing great guns in a little uptown theatre that

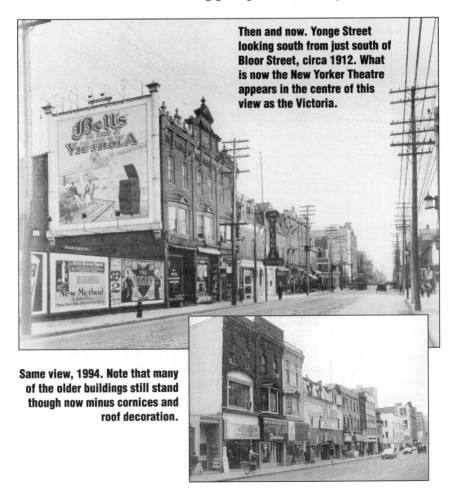

Then and now. Yonge Street looking south from just south of Bloor Street, circa 1912. What is now the New Yorker Theatre appears in the centre of this view as the Victoria.

Same view, 1994. Note that many of the older buildings still stand though now minus cornices and roof decoration.

Marilyn Bell meets Toronto's Four Lads after her historic cross-lake swim in 1954.

really hasn't changed very much since the days when Clark Gable, Bette Davis, and, no doubt, cowboy hero Tom Mix appeared larger than life on its somewhat tattered silver screen.

The two or so hours that I spent singing along with the cast of *Forever Plaid* (ultra quietly, as my wife, for some reason, kept insisting) were a couple of the most entertaining hours I've ever spent. There's absolutely no doubt in my mind that the music of the early fifties, especially the songs in the show made popular by Toronto's own Four Lads, *No, Not Much* and *Moments to Remember*, will be around a lot longer than that stuff they call music today.

However, I digress. While the major shows are performed in beautiful settings afforded by the restored Pantages and Royal Alexandra theatres and the brand new Princess of Wales and newly named Apotex Theatre at the North York Performing Arts Centre, *Forever Plaid* is going strong on the stage of the ancient New Yorker Theatre. Details on the history of this old Yonge Street playhouse are few and far between and though this is unfortunate, it's not surprising. When the theatre opened eighty-three years ago (or so a search of the city directory would indicate), it was simply another of the numerous so-called 'neighbourhood theatres' that began to appear all over town in the early years of this century. In fact, as late as 1954 (the time setting for *Forever Plaid*) Toronto still boasted a total of 116 theatres ranging from the tiny 325-seat Avon at 1092 Queen Street West to the 3,373-seat Imperial (now Pantages) on Yonge.

What we do know is that it originally opened as the Victoria Theatre (not to be confused with Shea's Victoria at Richmond and Victoria streets downtown) and over the ensuing years changed names several times; Embassy, Astor, New Yorker, Tivoli (not to be confused with the massive downtown Tivoli), Festival, and, finally, back to the New Yorker, the name it retains as the home of *Forever Plaid.*

BREWING UP A FAVOURITE
September 25, 1994

Every once in a while a little bit of 'old Toronto' in the form of a painted wall advertisement suddenly appears on the side of an ancient city structure. Take for instance the Coca Cola 5¢ sign high up on the old building on the south side of Queen Street, west of Spadina.

Sometimes it takes the demolition of a neighbouring building to allow an old ad to reappear. This happened a few years ago when work first got under way on the now-stalled Bay-Adelaide project as demolition revealed a nicely preserved Grand Opera candy ad on the old structure on the north side of Adelaide, steps west of Yonge.

Sometimes it's necessary to wander down a laneway to search out the past. An example of this latter scenario can be found out on St. Clair Avenue West where, by squeezing down the narrow laneway just east of

The original Mother Parker's Tea Company plant and warehouse was at 33 Front Street East, next door to the historic Beardmore Building.

Leaving the crowded downtown core in 1947, Mother Parker's was located in this sprawling plant on Castlefield Avenue near Caledonia before moving to plants in Ajax and Mississauga a couple of decades later.

number 1639, an intrepid (and thin) history buff can find an ad for Mother Parker's Tea painted on the old brick wall. At first it's a little tough to decipher, but after staring at it for a while (like those 3-D pictures elsewhere in the paper) the old fashioned logo eventually comes into focus.

Historically, Mother Parker's has been a member of the Canadian beverage industry for many, many years, but who was she and where did she come from in the first place? A conversation with Michael Higgins, Co-Chief Executive Officer of Mother Parker's Tea & Coffee Inc., at the company's ultra-modern Mississauga plant, provided answers to all my questions.

Seems it all started back in the early years of this century when Michael's grandfather Stafford Higgins and his friend William Burke established a wholesale grocery business under the name Higgins and Burke at 33 Front Street East, on the south side between Scott and Church streets.

At first the new company was content with simply supplying staple goods; flour, sugar,

Stafford Higgins (1878–1954), founder of Mother Parker's.

Courtesy Mother Parker's Tea and Coffee Inc. Archives.

coffee, tea, and the like, in an anonymous fashion to retailers who, in turn, sold to the general public. In this respect, Higgins and Burke was just one of dozens of other similar wholesale grocery firms scattered throughout the city.

Then, in 1932 Stafford Higgins came up with a plan to package tea under a 'brand' name. But, he pondered what that name would be. Ibex and Drinkmore was considered and rejected. Then one day, while Stafford was in conversation with a business friend, Frank "the chocolate king" O'Connor, creator of the extremely popular Laura Secord brand of candy and namesake of O'Connor Drive, the latter suggested, out of the blue, the name Mother Parker's which, they both agreed, had a nice, homey sound to it.

The original Mother Parker caricature (she always reminded me of a witch whenever I saw her while being dragged by my mother through the local Loblaw's store) was created by Stafford's wife. The Mother Parker on today's packages is a much friendlier-looking lady.

In 1939 the Mother Parker's brand of coffee was added and Stafford's son Paul took command of the company.

Note 'car card' on front of the streetcar, promoting Mother Parker's radio quiz show "Musical Memories," one of the most popular quiz shows in Canadian radio history.

Courtesy Toronto Sun, Toronto Telegram Collection.

As the large grocery chains began to crowd out the small neighborhood grocery stores, the company decided to drop the wholesale part of the business and concentrate on the development of products for the beverage market.

Today, in addition to the familiar Mother Parker's brand products, this family-owned Canadian enterprise (with Paul's sons Paul, Jr., and Michael in charge) has become the country's largest private labeler of tea and coffee and, as such, supplies the most popular restaurants and doughnut stores in the country.

And on the day of our meeting, company officials were still celebrating their recent triumph after having been selected to supply private label products to one of the largest food store chains in the States.

• • •

A special thank you to the nice readers who offered answers to a query I received from Mary Ball who wanted to know the date that the prototype space shuttle *Enterprise* flew over Toronto, piggyback on a Boeing 747. Friday, June 10, 1983. Can it really be that long ago?

FASCINATING ROCHESTER
October 2, 1994

Several weeks ago I wrote about a trip my wife and I made to Buffalo, New York, and how impressed we were with the beautifully restored mansions on Delaware Avenue, the bustling historic neighbourhoods, and the incredible number of grand and imposing monuments in the city's Forest Lawn Cemetery, the latter site worthy of a day trip in itself. A quick drive east along the thruway (not too quick, mind you the State troopers haven't discovered photo radar yet) and we found ourselves in the bright and shiny city of Rochester, the home of Eastman Kodak, Bausch & Lomb, and the Xerox Corporation. But there's more, lots more.

• • •

Rochester and Toronto share two historic similarities. First, both communities were, in their formative years, the sites of French fur-trading posts. Toronto had its Fort Rouille (better known as Fort Toronto) and Rochester, Fort des Sables. It was at these forts that the Mississauga and Seneca, respectively, traded with the European newcomers. Second, both Toronto and Rochester attained city status in the same year, 1834.

But here the similarities end. Our city was born as a result of a well-protected harbour within which a naval dockyard developed where ships were built to help defend the young British community against possible and probable invasion from the States. Rochester, on the other hand, owes its beginnings to the Genesee River and the fast flowing water that permitted the operation of grist and sawmills.

1921. Canada Steamship Lines ad for boat trips to Rochester, Thousand Islands, and Montreal (return fare $30 inclusive).

Postcard view of SS *Kingston,* a popular way for Torontonians to visit Rochester for many years, with a sightseeing biplane overhead.

As important as the river was in getting things started for Col. Nathaniel Rochester, William Fitzhugh, and Charles Carroll, three of the community's pioneer settlers who had left the comforts of the civilized American east coast and headed into western hinterland to make their fortunes, it was, in fact, the state government's decision to connect Lake Erie with the Hudson River via a man-made canal that was to assure the young community's bright future. Interestingly, the colonel was immortalized in the settlement's name (though originally it was Rochesterville) while the other two had to settle for recognition in the names of a pair of downtown Rochester streets.

Construction of 'Clinton's ditch,' as the Erie Canal was first called because of the support given the project by New York City mayor and future state governor, DeWitt Clinton, began on July 4, 1817. In that year Rochester had a population of less than 300. Ten years later, the $7 million, 363-mile long, forty-foot-wide canal, complete with eighty-three locks, had brought prosperity to "the young lion of the west." Rochester had grown into an exciting, bustling town that now boasted more than 8,000 citizens.

• • •

Much of Rochester's early history is still very much in evidence and that in itself was a great reason for us to spend a few days exploring both the city and the equally interesting neighboring towns and villages. Of special interest are the George Eastman House, the beautifully restored 1905 residence of "the father of popular photography," the Susan B. Anthony House in which the pioneer leader for women's rights lived from 1866 until her death in 1906, the Strong Museum, in which Margaret Woodbury Strong's collection of more than half a million common everyday objects of days gone by brings visitors face to face with America's fascinating past, High Falls, where a superb laser, light, and sound show plays out the history of Rochester on a 500-foot section of the Genesee River gorge, and, my favourite, Mt. Hope Cemetery, the oldest municipally owned burial ground in the United States and one of the oldest Victorian cemeteries on the continent. Dedicated in

High Falls, in Rochester, N.Y.

Modern day sightseeing of Rochester and environs is provided by the *Sam Patch*, a replica canal boat named for the legendary daredevil who, in 1829, jumped into the Genesee River from the 100-foot high Upper Falls, and, yup, he drowned.

1838, more than 350,000 souls 'reside' in Mt. Hope including the aforementioned Susan B. Anthony and Nathaniel Rochester, newspaper editor, statesman, and abolitionist Frederick Douglass, George Washington's drummer boy, Alexander Millener, and publisher and philanthropist Frank Gannett.

I made a special trip to one of Rochester's northern suburbs, a pretty little place called Charlotte. Also known as the Port of Rochester (the city is actually many miles inland from Lake Ontario), it was here that during the earlier years of this century the passenger steamers from Toronto called on their way down the lake to Prescott and the Thousand Islands. The familiar lighthouse, that has guided vessels into the harbour since 1822, is still there and I found traces of the wharves where the side-wheeler SS *Toronto* or SS *Kingston* berthed. And you know, I'm sure I could hear their whistles in the distance.

• • •

The friendly people at the Greater Rochester Visitors Association can make your visit enjoyable by providing walking tour brochures, B & B listings, dining suggestions, and the like. They're at 126 Andrews Street, Rochester, New York 14694-1102 or call them at (716) 546-3070).

FLIGHT PATTERNS
October 9, 1994

It use to be called Toronto Island Airport, though when it opened for business away back in 1939 the city fathers of the day dubbed it Port George VI in honour of the visit to Canada that year by the reigning monarch. It wasn't long before that regal name was abandoned in favour of the less pretentious, and no doubt, easier to remember, Toronto Island Airport.

That name sufficed for more than half a century until it, too, was abandoned. Now it's Toronto City Centre Airport, a name more reflective of the facility's proximity to the downtown core of our city, an important feature for many business travelers.

Though now overshadowed by its bigger brother northwest of the city, Pearson International (they haven't changed the name again have they?), Toronto City Centre Airport at the west end of the Toronto Island chain was built anticipating that it would, in fact, be the city's major airport. Another so-called auxiliary airport constructed at the same time miles out in the country near the sleepy farming village of Malton would only be pressed

1994. The old terminal at today's Toronto City Centre Airport was recently declared a national historic site.

Same view, late 1940s. Postcard view of the Toronto Island Airport terminal building. I trust the flight patterns depicted were only in the mind of the artist.

into service when fog socked in Toronto's waterfront. As the years passed, the majority of local aviators continued to oppose any attempt to make the Malton facility anything more than an auxiliary field because its location was simply too far out in the country. And, as they would tell anyone who would listen, the airport access roads were nothing more than cow paths. It took a world war and the desperate need for military aircraft to focus attention on the sleepy Malton field.

Now before you get the impression that the airfields at the Island and out at Malton were the city's first airports, history reveals that numerous private fields were in use long before the city got into the aviation business, even though aviator/politicians like Bert Wemp and Allan Lamport pleaded with the city to get with it and enter the modern 'air age.'

While their recommendations went unheeded until the Island and Malton fields finally opened in 1939, as early as 1910 private entrepreneurs saw the future of aviation and sponsored a flying meet on the Trethewey farm northwest of the Eglinton and Keele crossroads. It was here, in 1928, that de Havilland began assembling aircraft from parts sent over from the company factory in Great Britain. Before long both flight training and charter services were offered at the Trethewey location renamed De Lesseps Field after pioneer French aviator Count Jacques de Lesseps, a participant at the 1910 meet and the first person to fly a plane over Toronto. The influx of industry and housing forced the closure of the field in 1940.

Pearson International Airport, originally Malton Airport, had a control tower that looked very similar to the tower at the Island Airport. In fact, they were built from the same set of blueprints.

Other airfields in use before the Island and Malton saw their first aircraft landings and departures were located at Long Branch, Leaside, Armour Heights, a trio on Dufferin Street (Barker Field, west side, north of Lawrence, Canadian Air Express field, northeast corner of Wilson and Dufferin, and the Toronto Flying Club [TFC] field, north of and adjacent to the CAE field), on Sheppard Avenue, west of Dufferin (de Havilland's home after August 1929, and combined with the CAE and TFC fields the genesis of today's rambling Downsview Airport), at the foot of Scott Street (called the Toronto Air Harbour and restricted to seaplanes), and two small North York fields, one near the present North York Performing Arts Centre, the other on the east side of the lightly travelled Yonge Street north of Finches Corners (now Finch Avenue). Visitors to these properties had access to aircraft servicing facilities, scheduled and charter air service, and sightseeing operations.

In a sort of déjà vu there was for a short time a small seaplane base at Hanlan's Point close to where the modern Toronto City Centre airport is now located. Canada's first 'executive' aircraft, a Curtiss flying boat owned by the proprietor of today's Palais Royale, boatbuilder Walter Dean, operated out of the Hanlan's Point base.

• • •

This past September 3 the former air terminal building at the Island (oops, City Centre) Airport was declared a National Historic site. It is typical of fifty similar structures erected in the formative years of Canada's aviation history and today with a new lease on life as the airport's Administration Building is the only one still standing. A sad note. No city politicians were present at the plaque dedication. I guess their narrow mindedness on the future of the airport precluded any recognition of its past.

SWEPT AWAY
October 16, 1994

AND NOW THE OFFICIAL WEATHER REPORT
FOR TORONTO, HAMILTON, WESTERN LAKE
ONTARIO, NIAGARA AND GEORGIAN BAY FOR
THURSDAY, OCTOBER 14 & FRIDAY, OCTOBER
15, 1954:

"Thursday, cloudy with occasional showers and thunderstorms. Friday, cooler with clearing late in the afternoon. Winds light."

That was it. A few more hours of rain (it had been raining in the Metro area for the past four or five days), but it looked like it would finally clear on Friday afternoon.

Boy did the guys at the weather department miss on this one. Not only did the rain not come to an end as predicted, but a weather phenomenon never seen before in Toronto's long history was about to wreak havoc and misery on an unsuspecting community. And when it was over eighty-one of her citizens lay dead.

• • •

It was exactly forty years ago at 11:10 PM, October 15, 1954, to be coldly precise, that Hurricane Hazel slammed into Southern Ontario with disastrous results. Born off the coast of Venezuela on October 6, the eighth tropical storm of the season (in those days hurricanes were named after women – in fact, Hazel followed Gilda and preceded Ida – unlike the present custom of honouring both sexes) began to wander rather aimlessly before ripping apart the western end of the Caribbean island of Hispaniola, leaving 300 Haitians dead and hundreds more injured. Hazel then veered northward and after narrowly missing the Bahamas did the unexpected. Instead of heading out to sea, on the morning of October 15 the storm smashed into the American shoreline near Myrtle Beach. Again a change in course and now Hazel set her sights on the western end of Lake Ontario and Metro Toronto.

Throughout the day those same forecasters, who just twenty-four hours earlier hadn't mentioned the hurricane at all in their reports, suddenly decided we were in for a troubling storm of high winds and more rain.

Some of the many localities north of Toronto that suffered huge property losses included Beeton and Brampton, Holland Landing (when the storm finally blew itself out, more than 7,000 acres of rich farmland were under water), and in the ravine called Hogg's Hollow straddling the West Don River at the Toronto-North York Township boundary. To the west a trailer camp at Lakeview near the mouth of the Etobicoke Creek was devastated and seven residents got lost in the swirling waters of the normally placid watercourse.

But as bad as the property and loss of life was in these neighbouring communities, nothing equalled the agony, distress, devastation, and misery that assailed the unsuspecting citizens calmly waiting out the storm's fury in their homes on a quiet little street in suburban Weston.

A map that appeared in *The Evening Telegram* shows the location of the seventeen Raymore Drive houses that were ripped from their foundations by the raging Humber River on October 15, 1954. The dotted lines at the bottom of the view delineate the location of the footbridge that was to cause the tragedy of Raymore Drive. Today this area is Raymore Park.

What's left? The footbridge abutment is still visible, although it's now overgrown with shrubs and covered with graffiti.

Constructed on the flood plain adjacent to the west bank of the Humber River just south of the Lawrence Avenue bridge, Raymore Drive was flanked by dozens of small two-storey brick homes owned or rented by hard-working, blue-collar workers. In a few cases, elderly retired couples  had chosen Raymore Drive as the place to live out the rest of their lives.

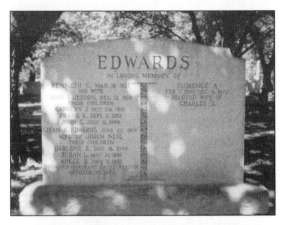

The grave in Mt. Pleasant Cemetery where nine Raymore Drive hurricane victims are buried.

In addition to the nearby Lawrence Avenue bridge over the Humber, Westmount, as Raymore Drive and the other nearby streets were collectively and officially known, was also served by a small footbridge over the Humber at the point where the river curved slightly. This bridge made trips to the shops on Weston Road easier. It was also to spell doom for many of the Raymore residents.

The days of rain that had preceded the arrival of Hazel had saturated the ground to such an extent that when the new storm let loose there was nowhere for the rain to go but into the nearby water-

Responding to an anonymous call for help, five members of the Kingsway-Lambton Volunteer Fire Department lost their lives when the truck in which they were riding was hit by a wall of water and sent careening down the Humber. A commemorative plaque in Home Smith Park, north of the Old Mill bridge, marks the place where the battered truck was eventually recovered.

courses. For miles around Weston all the streams, creeks, and storm sewers fed the Humber and so as the storm continued to dump its hundreds of millions of gallons of water, the usually tame river was transformed into a raging, unforgiving torrent, with walls of water gouging out new channels regardless of obstructions; obstructions like trees, outbuildings, concrete abutments, and even a few automobiles that had been swept into the fast-flowing torrent while attempting to cross the river further upstream.

Some of this flotsam and jetsam careened into the west abutment of the Westmount footbridge causing the span to fall into the river now sixteen to twenty feet above its normal level. In doing so the span, still attached at the east end, caused the river to be deflected from its channel and onto Raymore Drive.

Telephone poles, trees, cars, street signs, and whole houses, many with their terrified occupants huddled inside, were suddenly ripped up and sent swirling down the raging river. In all, seventeen homes and 1,200 feet of street were obliterated. Worse still, thirty-six citizens of Raymore Drive died in the split-second tragedy. Of that number, nine were in one house.

The site of devastation and grief is now a serene Metro park.

IRKSOME TUNNELS
October 23, 1994

Every day thousands of automobile, bus, and truck drivers, along with countless hundreds of pedestrians are confronted with one of the unfortunate legacies of the steam train's arrival in Toronto more than 140 years ago; those noisy, wind-blown tunnels on lower Yonge, Bay, and York streets.

With the laying of the Ontario, Simcoe, and Huron Railway tracks along the south side of Front Street in the early 1850s, it was obvious that from then on citizens would have difficulty getting to and from their waterfront.

Initially, the difficulty was limited to navigating single- and dual-track level crossings on those streets that reached down to Toronto Bay. However, as the railway business began to boom and lines reached out to Montreal,

Bay Street looking north towards the new railway viaduct and the Bay subway (underpass) on July 4, 1930. Note Witt streetcar on the *Bay* route and Toronto's (and Canada's) tallest building, the Bank of Commerce (now Commerce Court North), under construction.

Peterborough, Sarnia, and Hamilton, those few tracks began to multiply. Before long some of the crossings were up to eight and ten tracks wide. Serious accidents resulting from impatient pedestrians attempting to crawl under trains that were blocking the crossings became frequent occurrences.

To overcome what had turned into an untenable situation, in 1908 the Dominion Railway Board ordered that the railways raise their tracks on an overhead viaduct between Bathurst Street and the Don River, thereby permitting city streets to be pushed south to the waterfront via tunnels under this viaduct.

As this was a very expensive answer to the problem, the railways lobbied against the plan and, needless to say, nothing happened.

Same view, 1994. The streetcars (and trolley buses) are gone and the Canada Trust Tower of BCE Place hides the still standing (and still elegant) Bank of Commerce building.

Four more years passed and in 1912 a variation on the viaduct plan was put forward. This, too, was unacceptable and still more years of lobbying followed. An agreement acceptable to all parties wasn't approved until November 7, 1924. Preliminary work commenced the following day.

However, the first real step in correcting the continually worsening situation didn't occur until May of 1927 when a new Spadina Avenue bridge, replacing a dangerous level crossing, was completed. (Coincident with the building of SkyDome, that bridge was recently replaced by another new structure.)

Over the next few years, improvements to the situation continued with the opening of a series of tunnels or, as they were called back then, subways under York, Bay, Yonge, Jarvis, Sherbourne, Parliament, and Cherry streets. Each of these tunnels replaced a busy level crossing.

It was on January 21, 1930, that the first CNR and CPR trains began using the $40 million Esplanade viaduct. The newspapers reported that approximately 200 passenger trains *a day* would use the new viaduct.

With the trains now elevated onto a viaduct across the central waterfront, those dangerous crossings were history. In their place the city now had a bunch of noisy, windy subways to contend with, the ones we still use today.

Interestingly, when the Bay Street subway opened on May 1, 1930, officials decided to close the recently completed Yonge underpass and traffic bedlam resulted. One observer noted that downtown "looked like 'Scotch pie' – a lot of crust and a little jam."

• • •

While on the subject of steam trains, Ray Neilson has just released a new video titled *Railway Recollections Part 1: Ontario Lines in the 1950s*. This hour-long presentation, narrated by rail historian John Mills, takes the viewer back to a time when Ontario was criss-crossed with tracks and the steam locomotive was the workhorse of a vast rail network. Included in footage are views of double-headers, branch-line steam trains, long-gone railway stations, and much more. This GPS Video production is available for $32.98 at Sam the Video Man, George's Trains on Mt. Pleasant Road, Railview, and Den of Trains.

DEADLY STRIKE 3
October 30, 1994

Okay. We've gone long enough without a good Toronto baseball story. After all we are the reigning World Series champions. (Hard to believe it was two years ago last Monday that we defeated the Atlanta Braves 4 to 3, thereby taking the series 4 games to 2. Two whole years!! Then we did it again in 1993.)

Actually the baseball story I'm about to relate isn't a true Toronto story although the event concluded, and I do mean concluded, here in our city.

It was September 1935 and Len Koenecke, a twenty-five-year-old outfielder with the Brooklyn Dodger baseball team, had just been sent down to

The Long Branch Race Track became the Long Branch 'airport' on September 16, 1935, when a major league fly ball turned into a suicide squeeze. The area is now an industrial site.

the minors following a game in St. Louis against the Cardinals. After knocking around with several International League teams and finally making the big time, first with the New York Giants and later with the Dodgers, Len certainly was not a happy camper after his demotion to the Rochester Red Wings of the International League.

In fact, he was so mad that soon after he boarded the St. Louis to New York (via Chicago and Detroit) American Airlines flight, he got wildly drunk. So drunk that airline officials put him off the plane at the Detroit Airport. Koenecke sobered up somewhat and arranged to charter a private plane and pilot to take him to Buffalo. Irwin Davis, a friend of pilot William Mulqueeny, decided to accompany the duo and at 9:00 o'clock on the evening of September 16 the three-seater Stinson rumbled down the runway and into the air – next stop Buffalo, New York, or so they all thought.

After about an hour in the air, Koenecke again lost his cool, only this time he began fighting with the pilot and attempted to take over the controls. The ex-Dodger was considerably younger and more fit than the other two and soon the trio were engaged in a donnybrook that quickly became a fight for life as Mulqueeny and Davis attempted to subdue the crazed ball player before his actions caused the plane to crash.

Finally, in an act of desperation, Irwin beaned Koenecke with a fire extinguisher knocking him cold. Colder than cold, in fact. He killed him.

Now that the drunken passenger was out of the picture, literally, the pilot quickly realized the plane was well off course. Searching for a place to land in the darkness, pilot Mulqueeny saw the outline of a river, but its banks were far too hilly for a safe landing. Suddenly, as the moon came out from behind the clouds providing moonlight, he saw a clearing. Circling it several times, Mulqueeny, summoning up all his skills, set the craft down safely – right in the middle of the Long Branch Race Track, a popular chase course that the infamous Abe Orpen had opened in 1924 at the northwest corner of Etobicoke Township's dusty Kipling/Horner Avenue intersection.

An inquest was held and both Mulqueeny and Irwin were quickly exonerated when a coroner's jury brought forth its verdict that the pair acted in self-defence.

Incidentally, the Long Branch course remained active until 1957 when it was closed and the property given over to commercial development.

• • •

Remember Simon and Garfunkel's big hit record "Are You Going to Scarborough Fair" that 'made the charts' (do they still say that?) back in

1968? Well, they could be asking that same question today only this time the Scarborough Fair they'd be asking about is the one being held at the historic St. Andrew's Church at 115 St. Andrew's Road, Scarborough, naturally. Actually, this Scarborough Fair consists of two separate events; an old time community "bee" and "barn dance" on Friday, November 11, at 7:00 PM, and a dinner theatre show presented by Like Magic Productions and highlighting Scarborough's fascinating past (complete with some of the early settlers) on Saturday, November 12. The good ladies of St. Andrew's are preparing the meal so you know it'll be good. Both events will be held at the church (which is well worth a visit on its own). For show and ticket information call (416) 447-4895.

Incidentally, there really was Scarboro Fair (yup, that's how the old-timers spelled it) that was first held a century-and-a-half ago at Sisley's Hotel, a pioneer hostelry on Danforth Road just north of the dusty concession road we now call Eglinton Avenue. The fair was sponsored by the Scarborough Agricultural Society and it was very much a typical rural get-together where the best pigs, cows, horses, turnips, wheat, quilts, and bedspreads were judged and prizes awarded. The site of each year's event constantly changed, though in later years it settled down and the fair grounds in Agincourt became the permanent location.

As the township began to take on the characteristics of an urban community, rural activities began to disappear. And as they did so, too, did the tradition of an annual agriculture fair, the last being held in 1936.

Incidentally, readers who may wish to pursue more of Scarborough's fascinating history should contact the Scarborough Historical Society, Box 593, Station "A," Scarborough, Ontario M1K 5C4.

• • •

Forty years ago the Yonge subway opened, Marilyn Bell became the first swimmer to cross Lake Ontario, Hurricane Hazel was an unwelcome visitor to our city, and a bunch of youngsters graduated from Swansea Public School. If you're a member of the SPS "class of 1954" your presence is requested at a reunion get-together to be held at the Swansea Town Hall on Lavinia Avenue this coming November 18, 1994. For more details call (416) 392-1954.

LEST WE FORGET
November 6, 1994

Next Friday, November 11, is Remembrance Day, a day when all Canadians, newcomers, as well as those of us lucky enough to have been born in this great country, should take a minute to remember those who gave their lives in too many wars to ensure our freedom.

The first day of remembrance and thanksgiving (the second term was dropped the following year) was held, naturally enough, on November 11, 1919, exactly one year after the cessation of hostilities in the so-called "war to end all wars."

On that day, and at exactly 11:00 AM, all activities in Toronto came to a halt as citizens, young and old, bowed their heads to remember the fallen. And as the trio of bells in the tower of City Hall chimed the eleventh hour, officials of the privately owned public transportation company cut the power feeding the grid powering their vehicles and on all lines the old wooden streetcars glided to a standstill.

In city factories, the roaring of hammers, the crashing of machinery, and the whirring of wheels ceased as workers and management alike remembered those who did not return. In many cases, the dead had been fellow employees. In the heart of the city, where just 365 days before citizens had let their emotions run wild in song and dance, the streets were hushed in two-minutes of silence.

Over on Portland Street at the old Garrison Church of St. John, several dozen citizens joined two squadrons of the Royal Canadian Dragoons who had paraded to the little church from their barracks at the New Fort in the Exhibition Grounds in divine service of remembrance and thanksgiving.

As the day turned into night, dignified solemnity turned into fun and frolic with an Armistice Night Carnival and Community Dance filling the streets in and around the University Avenue Armouries. With special lighting effects, five French tanks, and three bands in attendance the nearby thoroughfares were turned into "a half-mile of ideal dancing floor."

At exactly 8:00 PM Lieutenant-Colonel William Barker, VC, DSO, MC, flying a captured German Fokker airplane, performed a simulated night raid on the city's Yonge Street only to be driven off by a barrage of anti-aircraft guns manned by Canadian soldiers. To hype the event citizens were encouraged to attend and "See What Toronto Escaped."

Scarborough's Courcelette Road honours the small French town captured on September 15, 1916, by the Second Canadian Division during the great Somme offensive.

Since its dedication in 1925 Toronto's Cenotaph, modelled after the Great Cenotaph in London, England, has been the site of the city's annual Remembrance Day service.

Later that evening a lavish Armistice Night Dance in the Pompeian Room at the Grotto Restaurant, 99 King Street West ("supper deluxe, inclusive, single ticket two dollars"), was deemed an appropriate way to celebrate. Even Toronto's premier hotel, the King Edward, celebrated that first Armistice Day and its sixteenth year in business with the opening of the appropriately named Victory Restaurant, with seating for 800 and entertainment by Romanelli's full symphony orchestra.

It's clear that the very first Armistice Day was a time for remembering, but it's equally clear that it was also a time to celebrate the still vivid memories of battles won.

But as the years rolled by, the horrible legacy of that first Great War became more and more apparent. Soon memorial cenotaphs began appearing in villages, towns, and cities. Here in Toronto, the war had been over for seven years before the Cenotaph of Canadian granite was erected, after much discussion, in front of City Hall (many suggested Queen's Park was a more appropriate site) and dedicated with a mixture of reverence, and pomp and circumstance. In the intervening years one of paper maché had to suffice.

Virtually every church, large or small, remembered its dead parishioners with names on a memorial plaque placed somewhere in the quietness of the structure. Cemeteries erected memorials where annual Remembrance Day ceremonies became, and remain, a touching tradition. War heroes remembered their fallen comrades with monuments and shrines, and city fathers named new streets in their fast-growing communities after hometown heroes or battlefields where their dead outnumbered ours.

Today, for many Canadians the accounting of our country's thousands of war dead and wounded are merely columns of figures listed within the pages of unresponsive history and reference books. For others, those figures were real people. To make their sacrifice meaningful, we *must* remember.

Five small streets in East York, laid out following the end of the Second World War, honour two Canadian war heroes. Vancouver-born Charles Merritt was awarded the Victoria Cross as a result of his actions during the Dieppe raid, August 19, 1942. Merritt was the first Canadian in the Second World War to win the coveted cross. Fred Topham, a medical orderly with the 1st Canadian Parachute Battalion, parachuted, unarmed, into enemy territory on March 24, 1945, to aid his comrades. Badly wounded, Topham was the first Toronto VC winner in the Second World War. VICROSS stands for Victoria Cross, WARVET for war veteran, and VALOR (though spelled incorrectly) is part of the simple inscription on the Victoria Cross "FOR VALOUR."

TORONTO'S FIRST CITY FATHERS
November 13, 1994

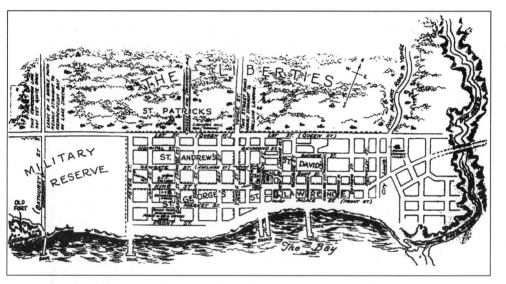

When Toronto's first election was held on March 27, 1834, the new City of Toronto, population 9,254, was made up of five wards and a suburban space called The Liberties into which the city could expand as needed.

Well, here we go again. For the umpteenth time since Toronto achieved city status back in 1834, its citizens will be going to the poles to select the people who will represent their interests at City Hall. So, too, will the citizens of other Metro communities as well as those of a myriad of other Ontario municipal jurisdictions. Let the games begin and may the best man, or woman (I think that covers them all), win!

As commonplace as municipal elections have become over the years, there was a time when such events were both novel and, as a result perhaps, more exciting than the rather complacent occasions civic elections have become.

Toronto's very first municipal election was held just weeks after all the necessary signatures and seals had been applied to an act identified officially as *4 William IV c.23 (6 March)*, the gist of which is summed up in the document's preamble; that is, "an act to extend the limits of the Town of York [our community's original designation] and its incorporation as the City of Toronto."

Prior to Toronto's elevation to city status in 1834 which, incidentally, made it the young province's first incorporated city (Kingston and Hamilton would follow in 1846), such municipal government activities as there were came under the jurisdiction of the magistrates of the General Quarter Sessions, a truly old-fashioned way of doing things.

There was little doubt that as the growth of the community began to accelerate, this traditional way of running things was quickly becoming unacceptable.

One way around the problem was to give the Town of York city status and a new mandate that would help deal with the problems of policing, road maintenance, taxation, and so on.

Courtesy City of Toronto Archives.

William Lyon Mackenzie has the distinction of being Toronto's first mayor. Whoever is elected tomorrow will be its sixty-second.

The act of incorporation declared, amongst other things, that:

Whereas from the rapid increase of the population, commerce and wealth of the Town of York, a more efficient system of police and municipal government than that now established has become obviously necessary,

And, whereas none appears so likely to attain effectually the objects desired as the erection thereof into a City, and the incorporation of the inhabitants, and the vesting in them the power to elect a Mayor, Aldermen and common councilmen, and other officers for the management of the affairs of the said City, and the levying of such moderate taxes [!!] as may be necessary for improvements and other public purposes,

Therefore, his Majesty by and with the advice ... etc., etc.

With the signing of the document on Thursday, March 6, 1834, the City of Toronto was born. Now it had to have a gaggle of city fathers and with that in mind officials agreed that in three weeks Toronto's first municipal elections would be held.

It would be necessary for the electorate to select two aldermen and two common councilmen for each of five wards, each ward identified by the name of a saint; St. Andrew's, St. David, St. George, St. Lawrence, and St. Patrick. An alderman had one vote in council and could act as a justice in the Mayor's Court. A councilman also had one vote but was not a justice. There would be no direct public election of the mayor. Rather he would be selected by the elected officials from the ranks of the successful aldermen and be paid an annual wage of not less than £100 and not more than £500 (approximately $500 to $2,500).

Toronto's first city hall, the former Town Hall, was located on the southwest corner of Front and New (Jarvis) streets.

Candidates for all positions were chosen by the citizens at meetings held in a trio of local hotels and in the court-house on King Street. Party politics was very much in evidence back then with the highly excitable "time for a change" reformers going up against members of the old guard Family Compact. Leading the charge for the reformers was none other than the fiery William Lyon Mackenzie, with staunch Tories such as Messrs. Strachan, Jarvis, and Baldwin trying to keep a lid on things.

And while the reformers attempted to have the secret ballot used on voting day, March 27, eligible voters (male only, of course) entered the polling place and announced their choice out loud. That was frequently followed either by curses or applause offered by those present in the room.

Contemporary newspaper accounts reveal that "there were but few black eyes bloody noses to be counted at the termination of the engagement." And when the city's first election was over, the reformers held a majority; seven aldermen to five with the councilmen split five to five, and they promptly selected the most vocal reformer, Mackenzie, to become Toronto's first mayor, a position he assumed on April 3 and held for just 303 days.

IT'S SANTA
November 20, 1994

The 1923 edition of the parade saw Santa riding a huge goose who, as the preceding day's Eaton newspaper ad reported, "had escaped being used as Thanksgiving dinner."

I guess for those of us who grew up in Toronto one of the most important events in our young lives, one that surpassed birthdays and even the last day of school (although that day was certainly important) was the arrival in town of Santa Claus who for some unexplained reason resided at both Eaton's and Simpson's downtown stores at the same time. Someone once tried to explain that one of the pair was just a "helper." Good thing we didn't have malls in those days. I'd never have understood the concept of a dozen or more Santa Claus helpers.

It almost goes without saying that Christmas day itself was regarded as the year's principal event. For me the day would start around five in the morning when my brothers and I would sneak downstairs to pillage a giant tree enveloped in gifts. Be that as it may, the day Santa first arrived in Toronto was certainly next in importance. Our parents would bundle us up in oversized snowsuits and boots (even though the jolly old man occasionally would arrive during a heat wave, we still wore those stifling suits) and head off for someplace along the parade route to try and see something. The adults were always good sports letting us little kids squeeze to the edge of the sidewalk where some huge policeman would make sure we didn't get hurt but still ensured we saw everything worth seeing.

Strangely, my most unusual vantage point for watching the parade occurred back in the seventies when, while doing a guided streetcar tour on one of the old Peter Witt cars for the King Edward Hotel, we got trapped on Bathurst Street north of the Bloor Street intersection. We weren't going anywhere so the operator, good old Charlie Price, and I, and a few of our hardier passengers viewed the entire two-hour-long parade hanging from various parts of the car, including the roof, where we saw everything. I never had a vantage point like that when I was a kid, policeman or no policeman.

The genesis of this afternoon's Santa Claus parade (that starts at 1:30 PM, has twenty floats, and will take more than an hour to pass any one spot) goes back to the earliest part of this century when store-keeper Timothy Eaton and some of his marketing staff thought up the idea of bring-ing Santa Claus to town (from

Santa rode into Toronto for the second time on his tally-ho coach, December 6, 1906.

A 1919 parade ad.

Winnipeg of all places) with just the tiniest bit of pomp and circumstance, then have the jolly old man suggest that the young ones, with their parents of course, visit him in the Queen Street store.

And so while Santa's annual visit to Toronto had occurred like clock-work every Christmas Eve for 112 years, in 1905 his visit was three weeks ahead of schedule with his arrival at 9:59 AM at the old Union Station. Disembarking from his private railway car attached to the Winnipeg train, Santa was driven in a new-fangled automobile (could it have been John Craig Eaton's car, one of the first seen in Toronto?) through the downtown streets (with children in hot pursuit) all the way to the brand new Yonge Street entrance to the Eaton store.

The following year, Santa arrived in Toronto Junction (the Town of West Toronto wouldn't become a part of Toronto for another three years) perched atop his coach-and-four. He headed downtown via Dundas (con-tinuing via Ossington which was part of Dundas Street back then), Queen, Spadina, College/Carlton, Jarvis, King, and Yonge streets once again arriv-ing at the Eaton store. Again it was a one-vehicle parade.

A few years later, Santa rode in a sleigh pulled by eight real reindeer imported from Labrador for the occasion. The Humane Society convinced Eaton's that Toronto's winters were too warm for the animals and that motive power wasn't used again. It wasn't until 1935 that 'bloodless' rein-deer began to pull the sleigh on a permanent basis.

As "the war to end all wars" ravaged Europe, the lucky ones here in Toronto continued to be entertained by the parade which, by 1917, had grown to seven floats and for several years ended with a big party at Massey Hall.

In the Roaring Twenties, nursery rhyme and fairy tale characters became popular float subjects with cartoon personalities of the day, Andy Gump, Min and Chester, Amos and Andy, Pogo, the Wizard of Oz bunch, Popeye, and others climbing on board over the succeeding years. Santa him-self was captivated by fast-changing transportation technology and his motive power took the form of airplanes and railway cars.

In 1939, another world war erupted. Fathers became more and more scarce and many households witnessed great sadness, but still the parade went on. And while gasoline and other forms of rationing were to cause some inconveniences, tractors could be replaced by men on bicycles and the recycling of float materials quickly became the norm.

Good times returned and the Santa Claus Parade got better and better. In 1954, the growing ethnic diversity in our city was recognized with floats recognizing fable and fairy tale folk from distant lands; Italy's Pinocchio, Holland's Wynken, Blynken and Nod, Germany's Pied Piper, Switzerland's

Santa Clause arrives at 'old' City Hall in the mid-fifties. Eaton's Annex (in the background) has been demolished. The 48th Highlanders' Band and CBC Television cameraman and emcee are on the store marquee.

Heidi, France's Cinderella, and Denmark's Little Mermaid. And it was getting easier to get to and from the parade; the Yonge subway had opened.

Then, in the summer of 1982, Eaton officials announced that because of the deepening recession it had been decided that their sponsorship of the annual parade would end. To quote the president of Eaton's, "Jobs are more important than the parade." The last Eaton's parade was held in 1981.

But the parade had survived wars and a depression and it would, no, it had to continue. Soon, members of the corporate community stepped in and under the direction of then Metro Chairman Paul Godfrey (wonder where he went?) a new, yet old, Santa Claus Parade was born.

PAST IMPERFECT
November 27, 1994

When I search various reference works for material to help me write this column I frequently come across stories that definitely have an air of déjà vu about them. Take this article, for instance, that appeared under the headline:

GASOLINE PRICE TOO HIGH, TORONTO CONSUMERS GOUGED

The story went on to describe how the reporter had purchased gasoline first in Toronto and later the same day in Woodstock and was astounded to find out that the out-of-town gas was considerably cheaper than that obtained in Toronto. To satisfy his curiosity as to why such a discrepancy should exist, the reporter interviewed both the Woodstock dealer, an independent, and an official of Imperial Oil. Of course, he got several answers including the independent owner's assertion that the big companies were trying to put the small guys out of business by charging them higher wholesale prices. He also revealed that his less-expensive gasoline was purchased from a small refiner south of the border who had next to no overhead.

The Imperial Oil official retaliated with the comment that the extra additives in his company's product forced up the price because it was better gasoline.

Imperial Oil service station at the southwest corner of Fleet (now Lake Shore Boulevard West) and Bathurst streets as it appeared about the time stories on gouging the driving public first appeared in the mid-1920s. An Esso station still occupies the corner.

Interestingly, in neither case were government taxes even suggested as the culprits for prices being too high in Canada. Why? Because the article I've just described appeared in Toronto's *The Evening Telegram* newspaper not last week, not even last month, but seventy years ago on September 19, 1924.

The heavy taxation of petroleum products had yet to be implemented, but that would come.

Sure enough, in the June 16, 1925 edition of *The Evening Telegram* newspaper, government officials estimated that the new tax recently placed on motor fuels by the province would result in revenues of at least $100,000 and that was just for the twenty-one days since the tax had been in effect.

They went on to say that the implementation of this new tax would mean the government could lower taxes in other areas. Ya, right!

• • •

Here's another "where have I read that before" story.

> Large resident groups are again at war with Metro. This
> time it's over a Metro plan for waste disposal dumps.

Reads like something that appeared in the paper last month, maybe last week? Well it isn't. This story is dated September 19, 1956, and while it dealt with the always present need to dispose of Metro's garbage, forty years ago the answer wasn't to haul the stuff east or north but rather to use one or more of seventeen sites located right in Metro. Places like the Eglinton Flats (Eglinton and Jane), Cherry Beach, Woodbine Park, the Scarborough Bluffs, the Toronto Brickyard (beside the Bayview Extension), the mouth of Highland Creek, and Toronto Island were under the scrutiny of Metro Works committee members.

The article went on to state that York Township Reeve Chris Tonks (father of today's Metro Chairman Alan Tonks) would never permit garbage to be dumped in his bailiwick. "The refuse should be shipped to northern Ontario," he declared.

• • •

Headline:

ACCORDING TO THE METRO CHAIRMAN A NEW 6-LANE
BYPASS NORTH OF THE BADLY CONGESTED HIGHWAY 401
IS PRESENTLY BEING PLANNED BY THE PROVINCE.

Sir Henry's Casa Loma wasn't even finished when the city reassessed it and his property taxes sky-rocketed 2,000 percent. A few years later he said "bye, bye."

The chairman? Metro's first, Fred Gardiner. The date? December 18, 1956. Nearly forty years later work proceeds on the new Highway 407, a toll road, located north of the badly congested Highway 401. And speaking of toll roads, in April of 1958 an MPP from Essex North was emphatic when he expressed his belief that toll highways were simply "roads for the rich." He couldn't understand why a driver should pay taxes on licences and gasoline and then pay to use a road. "With toll highways," he went on, "the poor will drive on one road, the rich on another."

And the stories don't have to be of the 'recent past' variety. Take for instance the following articles from the 'past past.'

> The fame of Toronto as a baseball city has gone abroad. Promoters of the new Federal League south of the border have commissioned a man to look over the city and have even gone so far as to secure opinions on likely ball grounds.

The date of this report was October 16, 1913. The upstart Federal League didn't get very far and it would be another sixty-four years before the American League Blue Jays were born.

Here's another example of "what's old is new again." This time the subject is the politician's nightmare, MVA (market value assessment). Think it's a new bug-a-boo? More than eighty years ago, November 16, 1913, to be exact, Sir Henry Pellatt is reported in a newspaper story of that date to be fighting the reassessment of his new residence, Casa Loma. In 1912 it had been assessed at $50,000 and in just twelve months city officials had boosted that figure to a whopping $250,000, and the place wasn't even finished. One year later his annual property taxes amounted to $600. By the time Pellatt had abandoned the place in 1923 those same taxes had risen twenty-fold to $1,000, a month!

HI-HO, HI-HO,
IT'S OFF TO 1938 WE GO
December 4, 1994

There's no doubt that this year's most popular video is *Snow White and the Seven Dwarfs*. In fact, since its release less than two months ago, North Americans have purchased more than seventeen million copies of this masterpiece, either as a 'must have' addition to their own video tape collection or as a gift sure to be welcomed by children, young and old.

While *Snow White and the Seven Dwarfs* is a brand new addition to today's enormous inventory of video tapes, the original film, the first full-length animated feature ever made, is more than a half-century old, having dazzled theatre-goers for the first time on December 21, 1937. Its creator was a young, talented man named Walter Elias Disney.

• • •

Walt Disney was born in Chicago, Illinois, on December 5, 1901. Interestingly, had his grandfather not detested the cold Canadian winters, Walt might have been born a Canadian.

The first Disneys arrived in the 'new world' from England in 1834 with Robert Disney settling in the States and brother Arundel opting instead for Ontario where he obtained work in a sawmill beside the Little Maitland River in Bluevale, a hamlet not far from the present town of Wingham.

Arundel eventually built his own mill and when not sawing wood managed, with some help from his wife, Maria, to produce a grand total of sixteen children, one of whom, Kepple, ran the mill for a short time after his father's death.

But Kepple hated the long, cold Canadian winters and in 1878 escaped with his two eldest sons to the sun, warmth, and supposed wealth to be found in southern California. While the sun and warmth were certainly there, the money wasn't and soon one of the sons, Elias, struck out on his own. After trying his hand at numerous jobs Elias married, and in 1889 settled down in Chicago where almost a dozen years later Walt, the fourth of five children, was born.

Newspaper ads for the Walt Disney feature film *Snow White and the Seven Dwarfs* which ran for a total of seven weeks at Loew's Uptown Theatre on Yonge Street in 1938. Admission, fifteen cents for children, thirty-five cents for adults.

As a youngster Walt loved to draw. As a young man he continued to hone his skills, producing his first animated short film in black and white and silent, of course, for a Kansas City, Missouri, advertising company. It was in this same mid-west city that Walt went to see a movie that would have a profound effect on his future in show business. That film? A 1917 production of an old German folk tale made popular by two brothers, Jacob and Wilhelm Grimm. Originally titled *Snow-drop*, the Grimm version of the ancient fable first appeared in 1823. A century later it had become *Snow White and the Seven Dwarfs*.

The idea of producing a full-length animated feature had first come to Disney in the early 1930s when he and Toronto-born Mary Pickford discussed the possibility of "America's sweetheart" appearing as the human in a film version of Lewis Carroll's *Alice in Wonderland*. In Walt's interpretation of the 1856 work, live action would be combined with animated characters drawn by the artists in his studio.

When another studio brought the film out first, Walt's mind flashed back to the film he had seen in that Kansas City movie-house many years before. He would produce his own version of *Snow White and the Seven Dwarfs*.

Work started on the monumental project in 1934. Nearly four years and more than two million drawings and sketches later, the film made its triumphant debut at Hollywood's Carthay Circle Theatre.

It wouldn't be long before Torontonians, too, would be lining up to see what *The Evening Telegram* newspaper's Helen Allen described as "the most delightful thing ever seen on a screen." On March 9, 1938, Snow White and Messrs. Doc, Sneezy, Dopey, Bashful, Grumpy, Sleepy, and Happy (oh, and that abhorrent queen/witch person) arrived at Loew's Uptown Theatre. The gang stayed for a record seven weeks.

(My thanks to the people at the Osborne Collection, Toronto Public Library.)

PAGE FROM THE PAST
December 11, 1994

I recently did an inspection tour of my local bookstore and jotted down the titles of a few of the many new books on various aspects of Canadian history that magically make it to the marketplace just about this time every year. I'm sure that the history buff on your gift list will find great pleasure in reading any of the following titles.

Take for instance *Just a Minute*, published by Little, Brown and Company ($14.95), in which author Martha Boulton presents the reader with a selection of short stories, each of which deals with a little-known event from our country's fascinating past. I was particularly intrigued with the story about Eddie Baker and his part in the creation of today's Canadian National Institute for the Blind. And then there's the story about the "Man of Steel" who first took flight in the vivid mind of a young Torontonian. And did you realize there wouldn't be all this Raptor-mania if Almonte, Ontario's, James Naismith hadn't tossed a soccer ball into a peach basket a century or so ago? There's lots more. Great reading!

Ron Brown, who's turned out several books on Ontario towns and cities that might have been, has recently authored a book on many of Ontario's pioneer railways that started out with great plans only to be absorbed (and forgotten) by one or other of the nation's two national railways. The book is titled, appropriately enough, *Ghost Railways of Ontario* and is published by the Broadview Press ($24.95).

Well-known television personality Knowlton Nash in his new book *The Microphone Wars* (McClelland and Stewart, $35.00) has, to quote the blurb on the dust jacket, "written a candid and unjaundiced chronicle of the tragedies and triumphs that have beset the CBC and its predecessors from the start right up to the present day." Of special interest to me were the chapters on the first Canadian radio broadcasts (especially the March 1922 event that originated in a small studio on Toronto's Wallace Avenue and was heard by a large crowd at the Masonic Hall, which still stands at the Yonge and Davenport corner, and by patients and medical staff at the Military Hospital on Christie Street) and the birth of Canadian television. Remember Percy Saltzman and Uncle Chichimus?

The prolific Jack Batten has added another book to his list of published works, this one titled *The Leafs: An Anecdotal History of the Toronto Maple*

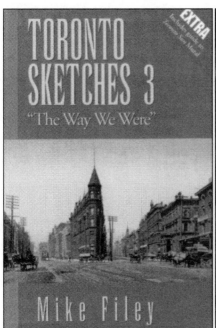

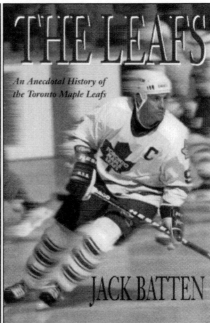

Historical books are a hot item as Christmas gifts.

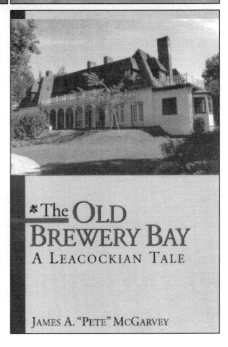

Leafs (Key Porter, $28.95). You remember the Maple Leafs; they used to play hockey here in Toronto. Unlike most books about the Leaf team over the years, Jack's book is different in that it gives the reader a behind-the-scenes look through words and memories of the players. And for those of us who were lucky enough to be introduced to the team via radio, the reminiscences of "Red" Horner, Cal Gardner, and the great "Teeder" Kennedy instantly take us back to those long winter nights mesmerized by Foster's voice emanating from somewhere within the Rogers Majestic.

Working at Inglis, by David Sobel and Susan Meurer (James Lorimer and Company, $24.95), traces the history of what for many years was one of the country's most important industries from its inception as Inglis & Hunter in Guelph, Ontario, in 1859 (needing more space, the fast-growing company moved to Toronto in 1881) through the hectic years of two world wars, completing the story with the company's long, sad decline that eventually led to the Strachan Avenue facility closure in 1989.

Former CKEY Radio newscaster and long-time Stephen Leacock enthusiast, Pete McGarvey, has documented the story of how he and many other Leacock fans set about to ensure that the great storyteller's Orillia, Ontario, home would not only be preserved but given new life as the Leacock Museum. *The Old Brewery Bay: A Leacockian Tale* has been published by Dundurn Press ($9.99).

And while I'm on the subject of works from Dundurn Press, permit me a 'plug' for a third compendium of my "The Way We Were" columns, the first of which was featured in the *Sunday Sun* some two decades ago. (Can it really be twenty years!) Titled *Toronto Sketches 3* (Dundurn Press, $14.99), the book contains more than eighty stories and also features a detailed description of artist John Hood's remarkable mural that graces the Front Street wall of the Sun Building.

Interestingly, one of the best of the new local history books can't be found in any bookstore. It's only available at select branches of the Toronto Public Library. Written by Lynda Moon, Barbara Myrvold, and Elizabeth Ridler, this fifty-two-page paperback, *Historical Walking Tour of North Toronto* (Toronto Public Library, $6.00) is the latest in the Toronto Neighbourhood series and tells the story of Lawrence Park, Canada's first garden suburb. A self-guided walking tour, map, and thirty-nine photos highlight twenty-eight residences in the 400-acre development that began to take shape in 1907 under the watchful eye of its creator, Wilfred Servington Dinnick. Information on where to purchase this book and others in the series, that cover Parkdale, Kensington Market, the Beach, the Bloor/Dufferin area, the Danforth, and Yorkville, can be obtained by calling (416) 393-7522.

MILLER'S TIME
December 18, 1994

L ast Thursday, December 15, 1994, was the fiftieth anniversary of the disappearance of Glenn Miller, one of the most popular big band leaders of all time.

The cold hard facts of history tell us that on a cold, drizzly December 14, 1944, Miller, then a major in the United States Air Force, boarded a small single-engine Canadian-built Norseman UC-64A at a small airfield near Abbotts Ripon in Cambridgeshire at 1:55 PM and with two others, former RCAF pilot John Morgan and Lieutenant-Colonel Norman Baessell, took-off for Paris, France, where Miller was to await the arrival of the rest of his band.

Glenn Miller and his band at Toronto's Mutual Street Arena, January 22, 1942.

Courtesy Don Pierre.

The Miller Army Air Force Band was scheduled to entertain troops who, just months earlier, began the liberation of the European continent.

Miller's plane lumbered down the runway at the Twinwood Farm airfield and vanished into the fog never to be seen again.

The half-century-old tragedy continues to be clouded in mystery. Was it simply a case of his plane icing up over the English Channel or was the aircraft, in fact, inadvertently hit by one or more bombs jettisoned by a returning allied bomber unable to drop its deadly load on a fog-obscured target? There are numerous other scenarios

Courtesy Larry Milberry.

Built at the Noorduyn aircraft factory near Montreal, this Norseman is similar to the one in which Miller flew as a passenger that fateful December day, fifty years ago.

and perhaps we don't want to know the real truth. And while his death may have been untimely, his music remains timeless.

Miller, who had knocked around the music business for years playing and arranging for bands fronted by such well-known leaders as Ben Pollack, Ray Noble, and the Dears Brothers, finally made the big time with a band of his own in 1938. It wasn't long before the Miller band was playing songs like *Tuxedo Junction, A String of Pearls, Chattanooga Choo-Choo, In the Mood, Moonlight Serenade,* and *Little Brown Jug* in theaters and ballrooms all over the States.

In early January 1942 an ad appeared in Toronto newspapers announcing that Miller would appear at Mutual Arena (until its recent demolition, The Terrace) on Friday, January 23, tickets costing $1.50 in advance, $2.00 at the door.

Within days, all of the allotted 6,000 tickets had been snapped up by eager Torontonians. There would be no tickets at the door. In fact scalpers were able to get as much as $5 for a $1.50 ticket.

One of the Miller fans in the audience that Friday night so long ago was fifteen-year-old Don Pierre who snapped the photo that accompanies this column on his Kodak six-dollar box camera. Don identified Eberly at the microphone, with Willie Swartz on lead clarinet, and Al Klink on tenor saxophone behind him. Miller, of course, is leading. Don turned out to be more than just another Miller fan. He now directs the fabulous Canadian All Stars – Tribute to Glenn Miller band that will be featured this New Year's Eve at Toronto's Four Seasons Hotel. They've also recently released a new CD that features a dozen Miller hits.

THE GLENN MILLER
ORCHESTRA with TEX BENEKE
FRIDAY, JUNE 14th
MUTUAL ARENA
ADVANCE TICKETS: $2.00 Each
Now on sale at Milford Ticket Agency, 317½ Bay Street, and Promenade Music Centre, 83 Bloor Street West.

Tex Beneke was fronting the band when it returned to Toronto in June, 1946. Glenn was still being mourned.

• • •

Canada, too, had a number of big-band legends, one of whom, I'm sorry to say, passed away this past December 5. I got to know Art Hallman when I worked at the CNE back in the mid-seventies. Together they brought back the Big Band Dance Tent where each evening of the fair Art and his band would entertain visitors as only Art could.

Born in Kitchener, Ontario, on January 11, 1910, Art was raised in Vancouver where he studied piano and saxophone. His first musical 'gigs' were on the CNR's popular steamship cruises to Alaska. In 1932 he became the featured vocalist with Mart Kenney and His Western Gentlemen and eventually formed his orchestra here in Toronto where he frequently performed at Casa Loma, the Royal York Hotel, the Palais Royale, and, as he recalled for me in my book *I Remember Sunnyside,* on the amusement park's Peoples' Credit Jewelers Sing Along stage. In the 1940s and 1950s Art was heard on CBC and CFRB and in the early '60s on CBC TV's "Juliette Show." When I last chatted with Art several months back, he hoped I could get him some work back at one of the places he liked most, the Ex. He was a great guy. Art and his music will be missed.

A MEMORABLE CHRISTMAS
Saturday, December 24, 1994

Choosing a subject for this edition of "The Way We Were" was easy; Christmas Eve in Toronto of old. Now, all I had to do was select just how old that Toronto of old would be. A century old? More? Less? Then I thought, what Christmas would have been the most memorable for the majority of my readers. Perhaps it would have been the Christmas of 1944. The fortunes of war were definitely improving for the Allies, and now, for the first time in many years, there was some good news getting through to Torontonians. Perhaps it was too much to hope for, but maybe, just maybe the Christmas of '44 would be the last to be clouded with news of turmoil, conflicts, and death.

Allan Kent, war correspondent for the *Toronto Telegram*, filed his December 23 story from his vantage point "with the Canadian soldiers in Holland." In it he states:

> There's no use in pretending that this Christmas will be a merry one for the boys over here no matter how hard the army has tried to make the day a little more festive with turkey, cigars and extra beer.
>
> There'll be patrols, but when they're over there'll be the command post where men can talk and rest and perhaps sing a little as Christmas morning dawns. A place where they can sit and think about the old home and wish they were there and hope to be there before long.

Back home, as December 25 drew ever closer, many Torontonians were still digging out from the record-breaking snowfall that had hit much of Southern Ontario earlier in the month. Starting with a few flakes of the white stuff fluttering earthward early in the evening of Monday, December 11, the unanticipated storm grew in intensity eventually dumping a total of 58.4 cm. (23") on an unsuspecting city.

A lingering effect of the blizzard was the problem of getting milk and bread to customers' residences. In those days the milkman and breadman, usually driving a horse and delivery wagon, was a frequent visitor on city streets. So, too, was the coalman and they all were hindered by snow-

Christmas 1944 is just days away and the Queen and Bay intersection remains clogged with snow following Toronto's record snowfall earlier in the month. Pedestrians, a Bay streetcar, and a coal delivery truck navigate the narrow cleared path on Bay Street. City Hall (now 'old' City Hall) is seen to the right with the future site of Nathan Phillips Square in the background.

clogged streets. As a temporary measure, local firehalls became food distribution centers. Ads were placed in the newspapers imploring people to shovel a path to the curb to facilitate the coalman's access to the chute.

What were the big gift ideas in 1944? Dealers reported that the demand for records, the 78 rpm kind, exceeded supplies, with the 'long hair' variety being the most requested. In fact, it wasn't just the 'singles' that were in short supply; albums of four and five records and selling for as much as fifteen dollars were becoming more and more scarce as the big day approached.

Tickets to the symphony concerts at Massey Hall were popular items as were paintings of pastoral country scenes and books. But with the latter, not all subjects were popular. Gift buyers were avoiding the war-type. People were sick of war. Perhaps serving as an escape, humorous books were selling like never before.

All over the city, sales of everything were up at least 20 percent over 1943. Perhaps rumors that the war would soon be history were to be believed.

Trees under which to put those special gifts were in better supply than in years past. Contrary to speculation that war-time trucking restrictions would curtail deliveries, it seemed that every gas station and vacant corner lot had some guy flogging trees for anywhere between seventy-five cents and four dollars.

And there was something new in decorations in 1944. With the coloured balls and silver ornaments manufactured in Germany and Japan out for obvious reasons, rotating stars and icicles made of a new material, Lucite (developed for aircraft canopies) were welcome substitutes.

For the special Christmas dinner, Loblaws had one-pound Christmas fruit cakes on sale for 60¢ each, "zipper skin" tangerines from Florida, 29¢ per dozen, coffee, 35¢ per pound, turnips, 3¢ per pound, No. 1 grade Delicious apples, $1.59 a bushel, two 24-ounce loaves of bread, 15¢, and smoked hams, turkeys, young geese, chickens, and rump roast all about 35¢ per pound. And police were reporting that a $3 bottle of rye was selling on the black market for as much as $14.

• • •

And while the joy of the approaching Christmas day was on most people's minds, a few concerned citizens were thinking ahead a few more days to the 1946 municipal election scheduled to be held on New Year's Day. In anticipation, an ad in *The Evening Telegram* advised that Ward 9 candidate Frederick Vacher, in an effort to help lost motorists, was promoting the placement of street names on the back side of all STOP signs while mayoral hopeful Robert Saunders was pushing for property assessment reform and accelerated work on plans for a Yonge Street subway that would certainly be necessary once peace returned. Saunders won, Vacher didn't.

• • •

With Christmas 1944 history, a very brief story in the Boxing Day edition of the same paper told of the disappearance of noted dance band leader Major Glenn Miller who had been missing since December 15, 1944.

RINGING IN 1946
January 1, 1995

Last week I wrote about the Christmas of 1944 and how for the first time since the outbreak of war five years earlier Torontonians could finally celebrate the festive season with increased hope that the Allies would soon be victorious. Those hopes were realized in May and August 1945 with the signing of treaties with Germany and Japan that formally ended the Second World War. With the world at peace for the first time in six years, New Year's Eve celebrations fifty years ago this year were sure to be special.

• • •

One thing this city didn't lack a half-century ago were places to ring in the New Year. Whether it was dinner and dancing at the plush Royal York or King Edward hotels, the Old Mill (where they still have supper dancing) or the Savarin on Bay Street, or perhaps a less extravagant night out at one of the city's many dance halls; the Palais Royale at Sunnyside, the Queensway Ballroom in Etobicoke Township at the mouth of the Humber (eventually renamed the Palace Pier), the Club Kingsway on the Kingsway just north of the Lakeshore and backing on the Humber (it started off as

Artist's depiction of the Queen streetcar subway. In the background is the Canada Life Building on University Avenue.

the Silver Slipper), the Masonic Temple at Yonge and Davenport, Columbus Hall on Sherbourne, the list is almost endless. And of course, we mustn't neglect to mention what was, arguably, the most popular "dancehall" of them all, Casa Loma.

With tickets available for six dollars per couple, hats, horns, novelties, and prizes included, visitors eager to greet 1946 in the splendor of Sir Henry Pellatt's "castle on the hill" would be hosted by Art Hallman who, as the newspaper ad described him, was "Canada's sensational new maestro." Art, who passed away last December 5, was starting out on his own having spent many years with the Mart Kenney organization. Art was to become one of this city's most popular band leaders and a good friend.

A list of some of the other fellows fronting big bands in Toronto fifty years ago would include Stan Porch, Ellis McLintock, Jack Evans, Trump Davidson, Eddie Stroud, Ferde Mowry, Bert Niosi and, who'll ever forget, George Wade and his Corn Huskers.

After climbing into bed following a night of festivities, citizens were expected to go out and vote the next day, Monday, January 1, for the new year's municipal council. The mayor for 1946, and returned by acclamation, was Robert Saunders, with Messrs. McCallum, Smith, Balfour, and McKellar as members of the Board of Control. Other now familiar names on the 1946 City of Toronto council were Aldermen Nathan Phillips and somebody named Allan Lamport. Both of these gentlemen would go on to serve as Toronto mayors.

Major municipal projects well under way as the new year dawned included construction of the Clifton Road extension connecting Mt. Pleasant Road (that ended at St. Clair) with Bloor Street and detailed planning for the Don Valley Roadway. The former we know today as the Mt. Pleasant extension; the latter, in a much altered form, the Don Valley Parkway, the first part of which didn't open until 1963.

As 1946 arrived heated discussions between the city and the federal government continued over the amount of money owed to Toronto following the government's expropriation of a parcel of land for a new Postal Delivery Building at the northwest corner of Fleet and Bay streets That's the building now being eyed by the Raptors basketball team owners. Incidentally, on January 16, 1946, Toronto sports fans witnessed a basketball game between the world's professional champion teams, the Fort Worth Zollners, and the Rochester Royals, played at the Gardens where the top ticket price was two dollars. Who said pro basketball is new to Toronto?

Staff working in the TTC's Rapid Transit Department had New Year's day 1946 off, but was back to the drawing board the next day as work progressed on the development of a pair of new subway lines for the increasing numbers of Toronto commuters. The Yonge line opened in early 1954, the *Queen* route was abandoned.

Those subways were years in the future and in the meantime the TTC relied on lots of streetcars (968 in 1946, to be exact) to do the job. Always on the lookout for innovative new technology, the Commission was also preparing to introduce a new form of transit vehicle, the trolley bus, the first of which would enter service on the *Lansdowne* route in 1947.

While on the subject of the TTC, transit riders off to vote that January 1, 1946, could purchase four tickets for twenty-five cents or simply drop seven cents into the fare box. Oh, that loaf of bread you were asked to pick up on the way home.

One other "so what's new" story from fifty years ago. Early in 1946, the Bell Telephone Company was experimenting with mobile-radio telephones. Today they're called car phones.

Courtesy *Toronto Sun, Toronto Telegram* Collection.

Big band leaders Art Hallman (top) and Bert Niosi were busy on New Year's Eve, 1944.

LINK TO THE PAST
January 8, 1995

Soaring over both the Don Valley Parkway and Bayview Avenue Extension just to the east of the abandoned Don Valley brickyard is the imposing CPR 'half-mile bridge,' the construction of which some sixty-six years ago was regarded by experts as unparalleled in North American railway history. Today, this engineering marvel is all but invisible to the thousands of motorists who travel under its seventy-five-foot-high piers.

When the Canadian Pacific Railway officially came into being in 1881 and for many years after, it had no direct route into downtown Toronto. In a manoeuvre that was to correct that situation, in 1882 the CPR acquired the Ontario and Quebec Railway whose tracks skirted Toronto well to the north. (This east-west right-of-way is still very much in use, though the city's growth now puts the route almost through the middle of the much-

Same view, 1995. Note Don Valley Parkway in foreground, Bayview Avenue Extension and DVP connectors under the bridge, and abandoned brickyard (only the "Valley" chimney remains) in background.

expanded city.) A few years later a line was built from the former O & Q tracks down the Don Valley finally giving the CPR its much coveted connection with the city's busy waterfront.

One of the bridges the railway was forced to build on its route towards the waterfront was erected high over the Don River flowing swiftly in the valley just west of Todmorden, a small community that developed near the present Pottery Road/Broadview Avenue intersection.

This bridge was 1,150 feet in length with its single-track bed supported by more than a dozen seventy-five-foot-high, A-shaped steel piers. For the next four decades, hundreds of Toronto–Montreal freight and passenger trains soared over the Don Valley on what had become known, for some reason, as the half-mile bridge (though my high school math tells me that the term quarter-mile would have been closer to the mathematical truth).

As passenger and freight equipment increased in both size and weight it eventually became necessary for the CPR to rebuild several of the bridges on their Toronto–Montreal route. When designing these new structures another fact had to be taken into consideration.

While the modern diesel-type locomotive was beginning to enter service on lines south of the border, Canadian Pacific's motive power experts still believed that the semi-streamlined steam locomotive was the way of the

"Half-mile" railway bridge over the Don Valley just before its replacement in 1928. Note lightweight construction and spindly steel piers. The busy Don Valley brickyard, with four chimneys, in left background.

future. It was believed that the streamlining would reduce head-end resistance thereby increasing efficiency and speed.

CPR staff then set out to design a new steam locomotive to fulfill these beliefs. The first of this new F2a Jubilee class of locomotives, number 3000, would have a 4-8-4 wheel arrangement with eighty-inch drivers and operate under 300 psi boiler pressure. (As it turned out only five of this class were ever built and they were less than a total success. Number 3000, which didn't enter service until mid-1936, is in the National Museum of Science & Technology in Ottawa.)

The railway's Ontario District engineering staff were fully aware of the planned upgrading of the rolling stock as they set out to replace the old half-mile bridge with a new more substantial structure. As plans evolved, of paramount concern was the fact that the busy Montreal–Toronto line would not be closed down.

In a move that would make railway history, it was decided to assemble the new bridge in-line with old structure replacing the lighter-weight sections with the new, more massive segments one after the other, all the while keeping the line over the valley in service. The time available each day to work on the removal/replacement phase was just seven hours, the interval between the morning and evening Toronto–Montreal trains. (Because the work was going on seventy-five feet in the air, no work was possible on days when high winds prevailed.)

CPR's new number 3101 locomotive at the John Street roundhouse.

The thirteen new segments would rest on towering concrete piers, with the pouring of the first commencing on May 1, 1928.

Each day, following the passage of the morning train (and weather permitting), workers unbolted a section of the old bridge after which a crane would lift it (and the supporting pier) out of the way. Then a second specially designed crane moved a new pre-assembled section into place where it was supported on a new concrete pier.

New rails and ties were laid, bolted down, and connected to the old rail. The bridge was then cleared of workers just in time for the evening train to rumble by. The interval between removal and replacement of each section approximated four days.

The project was completed on time on November 2, just 185 days after work commenced.

My thanks to Chris Kyle for details about CPR's ill-starred Jubilee-class locomotives.

See February 5, 1995 column on page 85

RAPTORS SHOULD DELIVER
January 15, 1995

If the owners of the city's new professional basketball team get their way, the Toronto Raptors of the National Basketball Association will, sooner or later, be playing home games in the hulking great Postal Delivery Building at the northwest corner of Bay Street and Lake Shore Boulevard West.

The idea of having the Raptor's stadium at the waterfront is somewhat reminiscent of a plan put forward by the Maple Leaf hockey team back in January 1931 when it was decided to move the team out of the cramped Mutual Street Arena into a new ice palace at the corner of Yonge and Fleet streets. (In 1959 Fleet was renamed Lake Shore Boulevard.) The reason for selecting this particular site? Ease of access. As it turned out certain financial arrangements dictated that the new facility be located on Carlton Street and a mere ten months after the January announcement, the Leafs played their first game in the spectacular new Maple Leaf Gardens. Talk about fast-tracking!

On the other hand professional baseball has always been a waterfront sport with a progression of stadiums near the mouth of the Don River, over on the Island, at the foot of Bathurst Street, at the CNE grounds, and now, of course, at SkyDome.

You may recall that for some time those pushing for an NBA team for Toronto were suggesting that the stadium might be located at the southeast corner of Bay and Dundas streets. It turned out that the site was too small to accommodate a revised basketball/hockey facility developers had in mind.

The focus then turned to the old Toronto Postal Delivery Building (in official documents it's simply the City Delivery Building) at 40 Bay Street where, with major modifications, a 22,500-seat, $130,000 million multi-purpose stadium could be built.

• • •

The history of 40 Bay Street, while interesting, gets off to a rather rocky start. The need for increased postal sorting facilities became apparent soon after Postal Station "A" at the east end of the new Union Station opened in 1920. At that time, the vast majority of mail to and from the city was han-

Work sheds of the companies building the new cross-waterfront railway viaduct occupy the site of the future Postal Delivery Building in this 1931 view. Note the new Bank of Commerce Building, the tallest structure in the British Empire.

The new Toronto Postal Delivery Building, still occupied by the military, stands bright and shiny in this 1944 photo. Fleet Street (to be renamed Lake Shore Boulevard in 1959) is in the foreground with the Royal York Hotel and Bank of Commerce dominating the city skyline.

Today, the Gardiner Expressway blocks out 40 Bay Street and the skyline has been completely altered, except for the Royal York Hotel (left) and the Bank of Commerce (if you can find it).

Proposed Raptor Stadium in the renovated Postal Delivery Building at 40 Bay Street.

dled by the railways, so it was only natural that mail-handling facilities would be located as close as possible to the trains. After a few years the new postal facility became badly congested. Plans to alleviate the situation surfaced on December 29, 1937, when the government announced approval of the acquisition of four parcels of land (one from the CNR, one from the Harbour Commission, and two from the city) at a total cost of $344,439 for an annex to Station "A."

A few weeks later city newspapers carried a story revealing that a new $1 to $1.5 million, 130,000-square-foot extension to the overcrowded Union Station Postal Terminal on Front Street would be erected at the northwest corner of Bay and Fleet streets.

A few weeks later another story reported that the project had jumped to $2 million and in an effort to help relieve the depressed work force, construction would start "at once." However, bureaucracy being what it was (is) the project remained stalled until June 15, 1939, when tenders for a new City Delivery Building were called. On July 29, 1939, a contract in the amount of $2,187,000, plus $26,385 for extras, was awarded to the Redfern Construction Company of Toronto.

Work had only just started when war in Europe erupted. For lack of materials and men construction slowed, eventually coming to a dead stop on May 28, 1940. (There's some suggestion that architect Charles Dolphin's building was too lavish at a time when money should have been allocated to the war effort.)

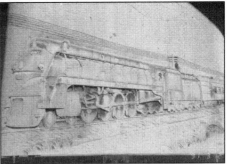

Carvings on the Postal Delivery Building.

The Department of National Defence got things going again on August 1, although now the building would be turned over to the Ordnance Branch of Military District number 2. A story is told that meals for passengers on the prisoner-of-war trains passing through Toronto were prepared at 40 Bay Street.

By the end of 1941 the new structure was essentially complete, but another year or so would pass before the Post Office was to share a small portion of the building with the military.

Following the war's end, the Post Office began moving into its new building and within a year all letters and parcels destined for city addresses were being sorted at 40 Bay. Station "A" on Front was reserved for outbound mail.

In 1977, sorting activities ceased at 40 Bay Street and the 2,000 or so employees reassigned to the new, more efficient South Central (Eastern Avenue) and Gateway (Dixie Road) plants. All postal operations and carrier activities in the old building ended a few years later. Forty Bay Street has been vacant since 1991.

Discussions between the promoters and city officials are ongoing and it is a given that the architectural and historical integrity of the building, including the beautifully carved, but woefully neglected, carvings on the east and south façades will be respected.

Starting in November, and for two seasons at least, Raptor home games will be played at SkyDome.

On July 24, 1995, following a lengthy period of negotiations, Toronto City Council, by a vote of 13 to 3, approved a proposal to convert the old City Postal Delivery Building into a 22,500-seat stadium for the city's entry in the National Basketball Association, the Toronto Raptors. The most contentious part of the deal was the exchange of a small parcel of land adjacent to the existing building for 450 game tickets and six days of public use of the new stadium each year, plus an annual payment of $80,000 cash to the city for twenty years. It is anticipated the new facility (to be known as the Air Canada Centre) will open in the fall of 1997.

SIGNPOST OF HISTORY
January 22, 1995

My dictionary defines the word *landmark* as "a prominent or conspicuous object on land that serves as a guide," a guide, I would suggest, even to the people, places and events of the past. Usually the object referred to in the definition is a building that more often than not has some outstanding architectural presence.

I say usually because at the northwest corner of the busy King, Queen, Roncesvalles, Queensway intersection is a building that may fall flat on architectural merit but is in every sense a true city landmark.

Roncesvalles Division, 1941.

Courtesy TTC Archives.

Now, while you're searching your memory for a landmark in that part of town, let me make it easier – think streetcars. Got it? That's right. I'm talking about the car barn and its adjacent storage yard. What gives this complex its landmark status is the fact that Toronto streetcars of all shapes and sizes have resided on this site for the past 100 years.

Interestingly, when I say 100 years, I mean just that for it was on this very day in 1895 that officials of the Toronto Railway Company, the TTC's predecessor, cut a ribbon (or whatever they did in those days) and declared the first Roncesvalles Division building open.

Streetcars, of the horse-drawn variety, had first arrived at the Queen and Roncesvalles corner in 1886. A half-dozen years later the recently electrified cars on the *King* route also made it to the corner. This conversion from real horse power to electric horsepower was in compliance with the charter awarded by the city to the new Toronto Railway Company in 1891. All routes were to be converted within a three-year period.

It soon became apparent to company officials that a storage facility near the western terminus of these two lines was going to be required. Plans were drawn up and the required structure was erected on the west side of Roncesvalles Avenue, approximately 100 yards north of the Queen Street intersection. The single-story brick building stretched 140 feet north along Roncesvalles, had a depth of 260 feet, and featured three bays, one with four tracks, the other two with five each for a total of fourteen tracks, thereby providing inside storage for seventy-five narrow, single-truck streetcars operating on both the *Queen* and *King* routes.

Streetcar storage capacity was almost doubled in 1907 with the acquisition of additional property behind the original building. At the same time, land on Sunnyside Avenue (the first street west) and property right on the Queen/Roncesvalles corner were also purchased to permit possible future expansion.

This was unquestionably a wise real estate move since the new, larger Peter Witt cars introduced by the newly established Toronto Transportation Commission in the early twenties precluded the use of the original Roncesvalles Division structure which had been designed to accommodate narrow, single-truck streetcars.

Toronto Railway Company operators and conductors pose at the entrance to the original Roncesvalles car barn, circa 1907.

In addition, the fact that the turn-of-the-century streetcars could be operated from either end meant that the old building had been constructed with openings only on the east side.

Obsolete on virtually all accounts, the old structure was demolished in 1923 to be

Roncesvalles centennial logo.

replaced with the present storage, maintenance, and office buildings, all of which are still very much in use.

Today, Roncesvalles Division is home to PCCs, CLRVs, and ALRVs, serving the *King, Queen, Harbourfront, Long Branch, Carlton, Dundas, St. Clair,* and *Bathurst* routes.

• • •

Roncesvalles Division gets its name from the fact that the original car house was located on Roncesvalles Avenue. That's a fairly obvious statement. What is less obvious is the real pronunciation of the street name, though Torontonians of Spanish descent are sure to get it right. Why? Because Roncesvalles (the literal translation is "valley of thorns" and pronounced Ron-ses-by-ays), is a small village five miles from the French border and twenty-six miles from the city of Pamplona in the Province of Navarre. Though prominent during the time of Charlemagne's attempts to conquer Spain (Roland, one of Charlemagne's commanders was killed at Roncesvalles), the fact that Toronto has a Roncesvalles is in reality thanks to Walter O'Hara, an early settler in the Parkdale area.

Born in County Galway, Ireland, O'Hara joined the British army and participated in many battles during the long Peninsular War as Great Britain helped Spain defend itself against Napoleon's invading forces. In 1826, he emigrated to York, Upper Canada, eventually settling on a farm in what is now the Parkdale area of the city. The names of many Spanish communities were still in his memory when O'Hara subdivided his property in 1856 and he used two of them to identify a couple of dirt pathways through his property; those names being Roncesvalles and Sorauren. Incidentally, he used family names for some other streets: Marion (his wife, and should be Marian), Geoffrey (son), and Constance (daughter). Fermanagh, a county in his homeland, was also his choice.

INSTANT REPLAY
January 29, 1995

Amazing, simply amazing!! Just when you think you've seen all the old photos of Toronto you're ever going to see, along comes another beauty.

In a recent column titled "Deadly Strike 3" (October 30, 1994), I wrote about a single-engine Stinson aircraft that landed at the old Long Branch race track in Etobicoke Township (just west of today's busy Kipling and Horner intersection) back in September of 1935 following a major airborne set-to during which one of the crew clobbered a berserk passenger with a fire extinguisher killing him dead. Readers will recall that the plane was on a charter trip taking a recently demoted Brooklyn Dodger ball player from Detroit to Buffalo when somehow the young man got a snoot-full and tried to commandeer the single-engine plane. After the violent mid-air mêlée the pilot, by now completely off course and confused by the inky blackness of night, set the plane down in the middle of the race track. The victim was quickly carted off to the morgue while the shaken crew explained the unreal circumstances to the local police force. As it turned out both the pilot and

Courtesy Elizabeth Sharples.

Pilot Bill McQueeny's single-engine Stinson aircraft sits roped off in the middle of the Long Branch race track following an action-packed flight from Detroit.

his travelling companion, who simply went along for the ride, were acquitted and allowed to return to the States.

End of story? Well, not exactly. Several days ago I received a letter from Elizabeth Sharples of Stroud, Ontario, along with the photo reproduced on page 82. In her letter Elizabeth recounts that her brother had read my story and it suddenly reminded him of a photo he had taken of the plane when he was a fourteen-year-old living in Long Branch. Seems that word of the incident had flashed through town prompting him to bicycle over to the track and snap a few photos. Later he described the interior of the plane as "having blood everywhere."

Following their conversation, Elizabeth got out the album and found one of the pictures taken by her brother. She sent it along hoping we'd all find it of interest. Thanks, Elizabeth!

• • •

With all the hullabaloo about the new cable TV channels does anyone remember the world debut of a thing called trans-Canada Telemeter in February of 1960?

Described as "pay-as-you-see" television the concept was the brainchild of Famous Players, the motion picture theatre people who marketed the idea in parts of Etobicoke because, as the promotional material described, the community had the right population base (150,000 – today it's 310,000) and "a great number of television sets."

One has to remember that at the time of Telemeter's introduction Toronto had only a single television station, CBLT (CFTO was still nearly a year in the future). Hamilton's channel 11 was on the air, as were two stations out of Buffalo and if you wanted to watch that trio an outdoor TV antenna (on a tower complete with rotor, if you could afford it) was a must.

The Telemeter concept was very much like today's pay-TV arrangement, though much less complicated since there were only three choices. Nevertheless, the theory was similar. The Telemeter signal was transmitted from the company's studio at 3010 Bloor Street West (north side, two doors west of Royal York Road) over a line installed by the telephone company to a small box that sat near the TV. The installation fee charged to the customer was five dollars and by the time Telemeter went into operation that cold Friday, February 26, approximately 5,000 residences had signed up.

Families could choose from three channels delineated as A, B, and C. For the first few days channels A and B offered movies, *The Nun's Story* on A and *Journey to the Centre of the Earth* on B, the films running simultaneously and commercial-free. The movies would spring to life simply by

This could be (but isn't) my brother and I glued to our seventeen-inch black and white television set waiting for "Hockey Night in Canada." Our home in North Toronto never had the opportunity to be wired for Telemeter service.

depositing a dollar's worth of coins into a slot on top of the telemeter decoding box. Any overpayment was retained as a credit towards future viewing choices.

Sports events were in the works and channel C was being held for local news broadcasts that would be provided free. The Telemeter host guiding viewers through the wonderful world of this pioneer form of pay-TV was former CBC (and the corporation's first) news anchor Larry Henderson.

Interestingly, in a newspaper account written just days after what was described as "the world's first permanent pay-TV system" went into operation, the Telemeter picture was described as being "free from atmospheric conditions because the film is transmitted over telephone wires which takes it out of the jurisdiction of broadcasting regulations." Oh yea?

As enthusiastic as the Telemeter officials were, the idea of paying to watch movies on television was premature and the Telemeter experiment (as the officials of Famous Players' parent company, Paramount Pictures, described the sixty-two months of pay-TV programing) ended on April 30, 1965.

TRAIN BUFFS GO LOCO
February 5, 1995

B oy, if I ever want to find out if anyone is reading this column, I'll just make a mistake with the number and/or classification of a steam railway locomotive. Trains are so confusing what with 4-8-4s, 4-4-4s, 2-8-4s, 3100s, 3001, and so on. Streetcars are simple. With them you've only got TRs, Witts, PCCs, CLRVs, ALRVs ...

Several weeks ago I attempted to describe the construction of the CPR bridge that soars across both the Don Valley and the Bayview Extension in the vicinity of the abandoned brickyard south of Pottery Road. In that story I wrote that the new bridge was being built to replace an older structure that was not designed to handle the mammoth new steam locomotives that were soon scheduled to haul Canadian Pacific's trains numbers 21 and 22 between Toronto and Montreal.

Soon after the morning train rumbled across the bridge, crews removed a section of the old structure and replaced it with a length of new, heavier bridgework that would be supported on recently poured concrete abutments. Also visible in this October 10, 1928 view are the old structure's partially dismantled steel support towers.

Warm weather and heavy rainfall (combined with an ice-choked Don River) turned the Don Valley in the vicinity of the CPR bridge and the brickyard (right side of photo) into a lake. This view was taken looking down the valley from Broadview Avenue, south of the Pottery Road intersection, on January 14, 1937.

Same view, June 1995, showing the Bayview Extension and Don Valley Parkway.

Everything was going great and then I slipped. I mistakenly referred to these new locomotives as being Jubilee-class engines when in fact they were Northerns built at the CPR's Angus Shops in Montreal.

Now, just to set the record straight, let me quote directly from the newspaper account in the October 19, 1928 edition of *The Evening Telegram* that described why the new bridge over the valley was necessary:

> Recently the company [CPR] built a large engine of the K.1 3100 class, the largest in the British Empire and for this reason five bridges between Agincourt and Toronto are being replaced.

With a 4-8-4 wheel arrangement (the buffs will know what this means, the rest of you don't worry about it) only two of this particular type, numbers 3100 and 3101, were ever made and, interestingly, both have been preserved with 3100 at the National Science and Technology Museum in Ottawa and 3101 in Regina.

In point of fact, the whole reason for my story had little to do with locomotives but rather was meant to describe the way in which the new bridge was to be erected using a technique that enabled regular train service to continue uninterrupted.

By replacing a section of old bridge with a section of new bridge, one length after another, supporting the new heavier structure on massive new concrete abutments that replaced the spidery steel supports, the railway was able to keep the morning and afternoon trains on schedule. The project was acknowledged by railway experts world-wide as being a true engineering triumph.

Actually, one good thing about setting the record straight in this second column is the fact that I can use a trio of photos that wouldn't fit on the page the first time.

TUG'S REBERTH
February 12, 1995

L ocated in the Canadian National Exhibition grounds is the Marine
Museum, one of several historic sites and attractions operated by the
Toronto Historical Board. The structure in which the Marine
Museum is located is the sole surviving building of a complex of many
structures that collectively were known as the New Fort, a title chosen to
ensure there'd be no confusion with the Old Fort (a place we now know as
Fort York) just west of Bathurst Street. The New Fort was constructed in
1841 while the memories of Mackenzie's ill-fated, but potentially explosive,
rebellion four years earlier were still fresh in the minds of jittery government
officials. Over the years Stanley Barracks, as it was renamed in 1893, has
served in various capacities including a short period during the Second
World War as an Internment Centre where 'enemy aliens' were processed
before being shipped to camps around the country.

Then, following the end of the hostilities, and with Toronto suffering a
major housing shortage crisis, the buildings were used for emergency housing purposes. It all came to an end when, a century and a decade after the
Fort's construction in 1841, the city decided to demolish most of the structures that made up the New Fort. For some obscure reason only the hulking,
limestone building that housed the former Officers' quarters was spared.

In 1960 the Toronto Historical Board moved its offices into the building, and a few days later the Marine Museum opened its ancient doors to
the public. In the fall of 1971 the retired Toronto Harbour tug *Ned Hanlan*
was plucked from the bay and deposited beside the museum.

Over the years the Marine Museum has all but vanished from public
view in an asphalt sea of cars and vans left by Exhibition Place visitors
attending events in the nearby Coliseum or Automotive Building. And even
when there are no shows the museum is so far off the beaten track that it
becomes a highly unlikely destination for visiting tourists.

And strangely, even when the annual Exhibition is going full blast, the
number of visitors to the Marine Museum is usually less than expected simply because the building vanishes behind concession booths, midway rides,
and tractor trailers.

Now a plan has finally surfaced that would see a portion of the museum's activities and artifacts moved to a new building to be erected at

Harbourfront. This plan will give the museum a much higher public profile plus a special water's-edge feeling that it totally lacked stranded as it was in a parking lot.

One of the most important features of the relocated museum, and a feature that will certainly entice tourists and citizens alike to stop by for a visit, is a plan to restore the coal-fired steam tug *Ned Hanlan* to operating condition, berth the historic craft next to the museum, and make it available for public tours of the harbour.

Ned Hanlan's bow is encrusted with ice as it departs from an ice-clogged Yonge Street slip in this undated photo. Judging from the cars on the quayside it appears to have been taken in the early 1950s.

The historic little tug *Ned Hanlan* may soon leave its home at the Marine Museum in Exhibition Place and return to Toronto Harbour.

The tug, which was built for the City of Toronto at the Toronto Drydock Company shipyard located beside the Keating Channel at the east end of Toronto Harbour, was named in honour of one of the city's most successful sports personalities who also served a stint as a city alderman.

In the early days of this century Toronto had an extremely active shipbuilding industry. Things changed after the Great War and when the *Hanlan* was launched in 1932 it was the first all-steel craft to be built in the Port of Toronto in more than a decade.

Ned Hanlan.

Toronto Drydock officials took great pride in pointing out that virtually all of the tug's component parts were of Canadian or British manufacture.

In addition to carrying out daily towing and inspection duties around the harbour and out into the lake where divers constantly checked water intake pipes and cribbing, the husky little *Hanlan* served as an Island passenger vessel during the months when ice prevented the regular ferryboats from leaving their berths.

About 1967, *Ned Hanlan* ran out of steam, literally, and the tug's future was uncertain. Its new owner, Metro Toronto, who had acquired the craft from the city following amalgamation in 1954, offered the vessel to the Toronto Historical Board for preservation. Thanks to the generosity of Montrealer David Macdonald Stewart and the tenacity of the museum's curator, the late Alan Howard, the necessary funds were found to move *Ned Hanlan* to its new home at the Marine Museum.

Money for the relocation project was approved under the Federal-Provincial Infrastructure Plan and work is progressing on both the construction of the Marine Museum satellite facility at Harbourfront and the restoration of the tug *Ned Hanlan*.

BROKEN ARROW
February 19, 1995

It's ironic that while tomorrow marks the start of Heritage Week it also marks the thirty-sixth anniversary of the death of a Canadian-designed and -built aircraft whose extraordinary legacy exists today only in books, videos, and in the odd scrap of hardware.

The genesis of the Avro Arrow can be traced back to the early 1950s when officials at the Malton, Ontario, plant of A.V. Roe Canada approached the Royal Canadian Air Force with ideas for a new jet interceptor that could, in the years ahead, replace the CF-100.

The first idea to be considered was simply a swept-wing version of the CF-100. That was followed by a series of other concepts including a radical rocket-propelled jet designated C-105.

Eventually, the RCAF decided on exactly what they wanted

Perched on the tip of a NIKE missile, one of the nine scale model Arrows is readied to be fired out over Lake Ontario. The Aerospace Heritage Foundation has a plan to recover these valuable treasures from Canada's aviation past.

Courtesy Canadian Aerospace Heritage Foundation.

defining the new aircraft's parameters in a document titled Air 7-3. The new plane was to be a two-seater all-weather interceptor with two jet engines for optimum performance and reliability.

Fulfilling those requirements would be relatively easy. However, the other parameters (top speed 1000 MPH, able to operate from a 6,000-foot runway and have a range of 600 nautical miles, possess an incredibly complex and advanced weapons system, able to operate under extremes of weather, etc.) were staggering and exceeded anything under development

The real Avro Arrow.

anywhere in the free world. Avro engineers accepted the challenge and in the summer of 1953 work began in earnest.

It would be impossible, within the limits of this column, to do justice to the amount of work that followed as Avro's engineers and technicians endeavored to achieve the seemingly impossible specifications established for Canada's new interceptor code named CF-105. But achieve those specs they did, and within a time frame that the aviation world believed impossible.

On October 4, 1957, less than thirty months after the first working drawings had been prepared, a huge banner placed across a pair of hanger doors at the Avro factory parted and RL 201, the first Arrow, made its debut as a huge gathering of plant workers, government, industry and air force officials, and a cluster of usually benign media types broke into thunderous applause.

Less than five months later, RL 201 roared into the skies over little Malton Airport. Everyone agreed Canada's spectacular Avro Arrow was a complete success. It's future was unlimited, or so everyone thought.

Well, not quite everyone. Less than a year after that historic flight, the entire Arrow program was terminated by the government of John George Diefenbaker. That decision, taken thirty-six years ago tomorrow, dealt a disastrous blow to Canada's once-proud aviation heritage. The final insult occurred a few days later when the five Arrows that had flown (plus a sixth that was 98 percent complete and more than thirty other Arrows in various stages of assembly) were hacked into small pieces and the debris shipped, under guard, to a scrap dealer in Hamilton. Virtually all documentation, molds, and related inventory materials were also destroyed.

• • •

A key component of the Arrow research program was the manufacture and test firing of a series of 750-pound Arrow scale models made of magnesium alloy from a site near Trenton out into Lake Ontario. Data obtained from these firings was invaluable in the development of what was to become the world's most advanced jet interceptor. For the past forty or so years these remnants from a time when Canada's aviation industry was unequalled anywhere in the world have rested in 250 feet of icy, cold water. Now, members of the Aerospace Heritage Foundation of Canada want to locate, recover, and restore the models and ultimately display them as symbols of a time when Canada was in the forefront of aerospace technology. Anyone wishing to learn more about the Arrow Model Recovery Project, or assist financially, is invited to contact the AHF at 1 Steinway Boulevard, Unit 8, Box 246, Station "D," Etobicoke, Ontario M9A 4X2 or telephone (416) 213-8044.

Enough money has been raised to start the search and diving operations will commence when weather conditions permit.

HISTORIC NOTE
February 26, 1995

I t's probably just a coincidence that on Monday, March 6, on Toronto's
161st birthday, one of the city's most endearing landmarks will be the
site of a special concert at which a musical instrument that for many
years was an attraction at another Toronto landmark will be featured.

Confused? Well let me be a little more specific. At 8:00 o'clock on the
evening of March 6, the Toronto Theatre Organ Society will present a Silent
Film Night in the Great Hall at Casa Loma. The musical score accompanying Buster Keaton's classic 1924 silent film *The Navigator* will be played on
the former Shea's Hippodrome Wurlitzer organ that was rescued from obliv-
ion when the theatre was demolished and eventually given a new life in the
Great Hall of Sir Henry Pellatt's castle-on-the-hill. Call (416) 488-1033
(days) or (416) 964-3265 (evenings) for ticket details.

• • •

Jerry Shea had been part of the Toronto entertainment scene for many years
when he announced in 1913 that he would build the country's largest 'show
palace' on the west side of Bay Street, opposite the City Hall, and just a few
steps north of the busy Queen Street intersection.

Shea was born in Buffalo, New York, in 1864 and with his brother
Mike built and operated several of that city's earliest and most successful
vaudeville houses.

About the turn of the century Jerry emigrated to Toronto and opened a
Canadian version of what the boys had started in Buffalo. Known simply as
Shea's, the simple store-front theatre was on the east side of Yonge Street,
just north of King. Some years later, Shea's choice of vaudeville acts and
silent movies proved so popular that a new, larger playhouse became neces-
sary. Selling off the Yonge Street property, he moved onto Richmond Street
East where he built a larger theatre at the southeast corner of Richmond and
Victoria and gave his new playhouse the latter street's name.

On April 27, 1914, another Shea's opened, this one having seating for
2,700 making it the largest theatre in Canada. Located on what was then
Teraulay Street (that section of today's Bay Street north of Queen) it
was called Shea's Hippodrome. Eight years later, a new Wurlitzer Opus

Casa Loma where the Wurlitzer organ from Shea's Hippodrome continues to entertain listeners.

558 theatre organ was installed in the theatre. Built in North Tonawanda, New York, the massive instrument cost Jerry Shea $55,000 and was reputed to be one of the largest theatre organ installations ever undertaken by the Wurlitzer people.

Over the next thirty-four years, some of the world's best organists, including Horace Lapp and Kathleen Stokes, entertained hundreds of thousands of visitors to the Hippodrome who may have come to see the vaudeville acts or the movie, but doubtlessly remembered the organ program best of all.

Following the theatre's closure in 1956 (the site was required for Toronto's new Civic Square and City Hall) the organ was purchased for $2,000 and moved to Maple Leaf Gardens. The installation was a mammoth task and the former Hippodrome instrument wasn't ready until December 20, 1958. That evening Don "Knuckles" Gordon entertained the Young Canada Night crowd with a selection of music befitting the season.

In 1963 the organ again became an orphan when major expansion of the Garden's seating area pushed the console, pipes, and peripheral equipment literally out the door. This time members of the Toronto Theatre Organ Society came to the rescue. Purchased for $3,850 the organ was disassembled (again) and the bits and pieces stored for the next six years in the secluded backstage areas of the Imperial Theatre (now the Pantages, the theatre's original name). There seemed little likelihood that the historic Shea's Hippodrome organ would ever be heard from again.

Then in early 1970, the City of Toronto and the Kiwanis Club of West Toronto offered the members of the Theatre Organ Society a deal they couldn't refuse. Casa Loma would become the organ's new home.

While society members initially set December 31, 1972, as the night the organ would be ready, the work program was much more complicated than anyone had thought. Finally, at a special concert held on February 12, 1974, the former Shea's Hippodrome theatre organ sprang to life once again. Who knows maybe they'll even

Shea's Hippodrome, Bay Street, where the magnificent Wurlitzer theatre organ was installed in 1922.

play Happy Birthday, Toronto, at the March 6th concert. Wouldn't that be nice, and fitting.

The former Shea's Hippodrome organ, with Don "Knuckles" Gordon at the console.

ARENA PLAN PUT ON ICE
March 5, 1995

Several weeks ago I wrote a story about the old Postal Delivery Building on lower Bay Street that the new Raptor basketball organization hope to turn into the team's new home court. Seems that the idea has offended a few preservationists who, I would suggest, didn't even know where the building was until a plan surfaced that would breathe new life into a structure that desperately needs some of that good old tender loving care. Don't get me wrong. I'm not a big fan of the 'Bitove School of Economics'; however, I firmly believe that the days of simply asking governments for hand-outs to save old buildings is long past. Working with the business sector to save and rejuvenate worthwhile structures, thereby giving our historic icons a useful and financially secure future, is the way we have to go. Take the recycling of the old Bank of Montreal at the corner of Yonge and Front streets into the new home, the Hockey Hall of Fame. I rest my case.

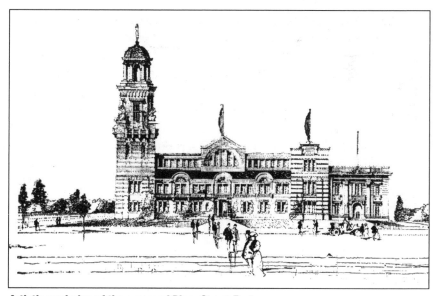

Artist's rendering of the proposed Bloor Street East arena.

Sorry, didn't mean to preach. What prompts my return to the subject of the possible transformation of the Postal Delivery Building into a sports facility was an item I found while scanning the July 15, 1909 edition of the *The Evening Telegram* newspaper. (No, our delivery boy isn't slow, the old papers are on microfilm in the *Sun* library.)

The headline of the article announced that some local businessmen

WANT TO BUILD NEW ARENA

with a sub-heading that went on

BUT CITIZENS OBJECT

While basketball, the creation of Ontario-born James Naismith (1861–1939), was popular in the Toronto of 1909 both in the school system and at the various local YMCA branches, a professional facility wasn't yet deemed a necessity. The arena in the newspaper article was to be of the ice skating variety. The site of the new arena complex was to be on a large parcel of land on the north side of Bloor Street a hundred or so yards east of Yonge running north to Rosedale Valley Road. The property had been acquired by the Board of Education for a technical school that never materialized. (Perhaps the site was too far north. The new Central Technical School opened further downtown on Harbord Street in September 1915.)

The promoters envisioned a large structure with a trio of rink surfaces (all with artificial ice), one devoted to children, one to "ladies and gents," and the third (and at eighty feet by two hundred feet, the largest) for hockey matches. The latter rink could be converted into a convention hall with seating for 10,000. There would also be a so-called symphony hall with seating for 1,800, dressing rooms, a pair of curling rinks, and an indoor gentlemen's riding club.

The foes of the $240,000 project included members of the nearby St. Paul's and Central Methodist Churches, staff of both Moulton and St. Margaret's Colleges for Women, the directors and doctors of the Incurable Children's Hospital, and, not surprisingly, a host of private citizens residing in the many large houses that flanked both sides of Bloor Street, east and west of Yonge Street. It was a very different corner eighty-six years ago.

Needless to say, the arena never got off the drawing board.

• • •

I recently received a copy of a new booklet prepared by Owen Thomas that provides facts about a little-known facet of our province's fascinating history. *Niagara's Freedom Trail* is a skillfully researched guide to African-Canadian history throughout the Niagara Peninsula. Included in Owen's booklet are stories about the Fort Erie slave-crossing site at the terminus of the Underground Railway, the Solomon Moseby affair, the Battle of Slabtown, and the legendary Harriet Tubman. Why not pick up a copy of the guide, put it into your car glovebox, and when the weather gets better head out and rediscover the Niagara Peninsula.

For details on receiving a copy of the booklet call Region Niagara Tourist Council at 1-(800) 263-2988.

Follow the North Star
The guiding light of the Underground Railroad

Niagara's Freedom Trail
by: Owen A. Thomas

A Guide to African-Canadian History on the Niagara Peninsula

For the Region Niagara Tourist Council
Prepared and Published with the Assistance of the Ontario Heritage Foundation

ERIN GO BRAGH!
March 12, 1995

Next Friday there'll be just two nationalities in this tired old world; those who are Irish and those who wish they were. Let me be the first to wish you a happy St. Patrick's Day. And while we're on the subject of Irish heritage, did you know that by the mid-1800s the Irish actually outnumbered both the English and Scots in the fast-growing city of Toronto? Many of Toronto's pioneer businessmen like Timothy Eaton were born on the "Emerald Isle," while others like Eugene O'Keefe and Frank O'Connor were born of Irish parentage. Several of the city's pre-twentieth-century mayors were Irish including the second person to hold that office, Robert Baldwin Sullivan. And it certainly didn't hurt your chances to become a city policeman in the 1800s if your background happened to be Irish.

• • •

While most Torontonians are familiar with today's sprawling St. Lawrence Market at the corner of Front and Jarvis streets, I bet few have even heard of the city's St. Patrick's Market. And while it's a fact of history that the St. Lawrence Market holds the distinction of being Toronto's first (having been proclaimed into being by Lieutenant-Governor Peter Hunter in 1803), the establishment of the St. Patrick's Market just thirty-three years later made it the city's second and the first market west of Yonge Street. It was called St. Patrick's Market simply because it was located in St. Patrick's Ward, one of the original five wards (Saints Patrick, David, George, Andrews, and Lawrence) into which the city had been divided by the terms of the 1834 Act of Incorporation.

The "father" of the St. Patrick's Market was prominent local landowner D'Arcy Boulton, Jr., who, sometime in 1836, sat at his desk in the Grange (now part of the Art Gallery of Ontario) and penned a letter to civic officials offering them a parcel of land fronting on Lot Street in the westernmost hinterland of the two-year-old city with the proviso that a market be erected thereon.

There's no question that Boulton's offer wasn't made just because he was a nice guy. Financial setbacks had made it imperative that Boulton sell

Timothy Eaton (left) and Frank O'Connor, two prominent Toronto businessmen with Irish roots.

portions of the 100-acre lot (it's now called Queen) that he had acquired in 1808 for £350 ($1,650). In a shrewd marketing move he offered land free of charge for both a market and church believing that these two amenities would enhance the salability of the surrounding property. Thus it was that in 1836 the original St. Patrick's Market opened, followed nine years later by the consecration of the nearby Church of St. George the Martyr.

Interestingly, the terms of Boulton's original 1836 proposal continue in effect with the city head leasing the site on the north side of Queen just west of McCaul to Queen-St. Patrick Inc. who operate the Queen Street market. A small park behind the market building retains the St. Patrick identification in its title.

• • •

In today's multicultural Toronto, St. Patrick's Day comes and goes leaving few complications in its wake. But that wasn't always the case. Take the year 1878 for instance. Back then Torontonians had nothing but contempt for the Fenian Brotherhood's plan to rid Ireland of British rule through the use of deadly force. As a result, when O'Donovan Rossa who, as secretary and spokesperson for the Brotherhood's so-called "skirmishing fund," agreed to address local sympathizers during his North American speaking tour the fuse was lit. Rossa was scheduled to lecture on March 19 (St. Patrick's Day

The original St. Patrick's Market, on Queen Street West near McCaul, was a wooden structure that was replaced by this brick structure in 1854. Today, the market occupies a modern structure.

that year fell on a Sunday, a day devoted exclusively to religious pursuits), and, fully aware of possible threats on his life, he arrived at the old St. Patrick's Hall (upstairs in the St. Lawrence Hall) in disguise. Sure enough a crowd gathered outside the building and began showering it with stones. The police moved in and dispersed the crowd only to have it reform up the street at the Adelaide corner. In the meantime Rossa escaped after having once again changed clothing. The fired-up crowd then made a beeline for Owen Cosgrave's tavern at the corner of Queen and Dummer (now St. Patrick) streets, a known haunt of Irish sympathizers. Within minutes the place was in shambles, the brick roadway and sidewalks making for an endless source of ammunition.

TUNNEL VISION
March 19, 1995

Courtesy Toronto Harbour Commission Archives.

In 1897 the dangers of the York Street crossing were eliminated with the opening of this temporary bridge that was replaced years later by an underpass. Note the old Union Station to the left of the bridge and the new station to the extreme right. The abandoned ship in the foreground proves that anything that didn't move could be useful as landfill for the city's emerging waterfront.

For decades they tried to get the thing built. Now, in just a few short days, it'll be gone. What, you may ask, is he going on about? Well, anyone who travels to and from downtown through the long, cold, dark York Street underpass south of Front Street will know immediately because for the next week or so you can't. That's because as part of the redevelopment of the city's central waterfront area much of that underpass is being demolished.

• • •

When the city entered the railway era on May 16, 1853, it also entered into a seemingly endless period of conflict with the railways, as city officials tried time and time again to win back unobstructed access to Toronto's developing waterfront.

It was on that spring day 142 years ago that the Ontario, Simcoe, and Huron Railway's balloon-stacked locomotive number 2 (christened *Toronto* in honour of the city of its manufacture), with Master Mechanic William Hackett at the controls, moved slowly away from the little passenger station at the foot of Bay Street. The train, consisting of two wooden boxcars, a combination freight/smoking car, and a single passenger coach all under the watchful eye of conductor John Harvie, chugged westerly along a new set of tracks laid on the south of Front Street on a routing that would take the province's first train to a little place north of the city called Machell's Corners, a community that a year later would be renamed Aurora.

On January 1, 1855, that pioneer line made it all the way north to a small port on the south shore of Georgian Bay, a place we now call Collingwood.

As the years went by competing railways began laying their own tracks across the city's waterfront as they attempted to get their trains as close as possible to the lucrative shipping wharves or drop cargo at the numerous coal and lumber yards that stretched all along the north shore of the harbour. In fact, to accommodate this ever-widening rail corridor it became necessary to create new land by filling in the waterfront with street sweepings (certainly a nicer word than garbage) and dredged material from the

The York Street subway under the viaduct opened on September 15, 1930. This view was taken twenty-two years later.

depths of Toronto Harbour. Slowly but surely the city was extended further and further into the bay until officials took steps to halt this uncontrolled expansion.

Certainly the most serious problem that resulted from the widening of the cross-waterfront rail corridor was the danger faced by both pedestrians and horse-drawn vehicles as they attempted to traverse the multitude of busy rail lines. While some protection was afforded by the bobby-helmeted

A large portion of the York Street underpass lies as rubble (to the right) just days after the demolition project started on March 23, 1995.

policemen dispatched to the waterfront on busy summer days, for the most part the crossings at the foot of Jarvis, Church, Yonge, Bay, and Front streets were death traps. The newspapers of the day are filled with stories about men, women, and children killed or maimed as they braved these hazardous crossings.

Recognizing the growing seriousness of the situation, city fathers and railway officials agreed in April of 1905 that the city streets and rail crossings should be separated. Two years later, in a report prepared by the City Engineer, it was recommended that an earth-fill viaduct be constructed the length of the Esplanade with subways for pedestrian and vehicular traffic provided at York, Bay, Yonge, Scott, Church, Jarvis, George, Frederick, Sherbourne, Princess, Berkeley, and Parliament streets. Nothing happened.

In fact, another decade was to go by before the city's new viaduct even began to take shape. And when the $28 million project was finally completed in 1930 only six of the original dozen underpasses were constructed. Because it was an integral part of the city's new Union Station complex which was built coincident with the viaduct project, the underpass at York Street was the last to be opened to traffic, an event that took place with little fanfare on September 15, 1930. And thanks to co-operative efforts by the City of Toronto, Marathon Realty, the Metro Toronto Convention Centre, and the Waterfront Regeneration Trust, by this time next week most of it will have vanished.

REIGN IN SPAIN
March 26, 1995

As I sit at my desk preparing this column for the March 26 edition of the paper, it would appear that the so-called "turbot war" has been 'scaled' down and that talk and compromise will win the day.

This confrontation with Spain is in direct contrast with the way things were some 187 years ago when a future Torontonian, nineteen-year-old Walter O'Hara, wearing the uniform of the 1st Line Regiment of Foot in the British army, took up arms to help free Spain from that bully, Napoleon Bonaparte, Emperor of France.

The history books refer to the confrontation as the

Walter O'Hara, veteran of the Spanish Peninsular War.

Peninsular War, taking place as it did from 1808 to 1814 all throughout the Spanish peninsula. It all started when France, long at loggerheads with Great Britain, tried to starve the British by having others refuse to trade with her. When Portugal refused to go along with Napoleon's directive, the Emperor dispatched French troops to carry out his orders. First, though, he got Spanish assurance that his army could take a short cut across the Spanish peninsula.

No sooner had Napoleon invaded Portugal that he decided that he wanted to rule Spain as well. Well that did it. Britain was determined to rid both Portugal and Spain of this guy, Napoleon, for good.

Back to Walter O'Hara. He was born in Dublin and educated at that city's famous Trinity College following which he embarked on a military

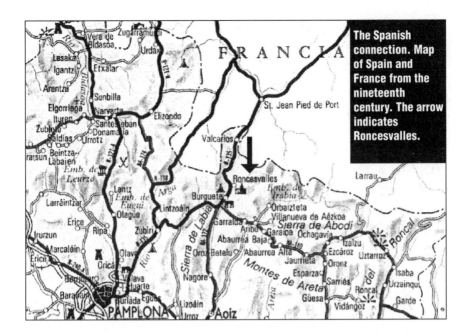

career. His timing was perfect for with the outbreak of the Peninsular War, O'Hara found himself in the thick of battle. In fact, he was twice wounded and, as some sources suggest, was also taken prisoner at the fierce battle of the Nive River.

A dozen years after the cessation of hostilities, O'Hara decided to seek his future in British North America emigrating to Upper Canada (Ontario) in 1826, settling on a farm well west of the Town of York, a location that today would be described as in the Parkdale area of Toronto.

Roncesvalles and Sorauren street signs in Toronto. Marion was O'Hara's wife, although she spelled it Marian.

O'Hara's military experience resulted in his appointment as assistant adjutant-general of the provincial militia, a position that brought with it the rank of colonel. In 1837, when the firebrand William Lyon Mackenzie decided to march down Yonge Street and overthrow the government by force, it was only natural that Colonel O'Hara, veteran of the fierce Peninsular War, would be called on to defend his adopted city against a new enemy.

After Mackenzie's ill-starred rebellion fizzled out, O'Hara returned to his farm where he lived in quiet obscurity. In 1856, he decided to subdivide some of his property and in doing so laid out a series of new streets. Some he named after family members: Geoffrey for his son, Constance for his daughter, Marion for his wife (though she spelled her name Marian), Fermanagh in recognition of his homeland, and others that recalled vivid memories of battles in Spain near the small northern communities of Roncesvalles (roll the "r," ron-ces-by-ez) and Sorauren.

Walter O'Hara died at his residence, West Lodge, in 1874.

• • •

I've recently come across several new books that I'm sure would be well received by anyone the least bit interested in history. The first, *Today in History*, by CBC Radio personality Bob Johnstone (Warwick Publishing, $18.95), deals with world events, one for each day of the year. Another, *Working at Inglis*, by David Sobel and Susan Meurer (James Lorimer and Company, $24.95) tells the bittersweet story behind the rise and fall of one of this city's oldest companies. *Just a Moment*, by Marsha Boulton (Little, Brown and Company, $14.95) provides the reader with dozens of stories documenting little-known Canadian facts (Superman was a Canadian creation, the McIntosh apple happened by accident, a Canadian soldier in the First World War, blinded by sniper fire, helped establish the CNIB, etc., etc.). *Ladies and Gentlemen ... Mr. Harry 'Red' Foster*, by Paul E. Lewis (NC Press, $24.95) tells the story of a fascinating Canadian who, through his radio broadcasts and promotions in the 1930s and '40s, was as well known as any media personality today. His legacy is the Canadian Special Olympics which he helped establish a quarter-century ago.

TOWER TURNS TWENTY
Sunday, April 2, 1995

I t's funny how events we perceive as happening just a few weeks ago turn out to have actually occurred months, years, even decades in the past. A case in point: Were you among the thousands who peered skyward to watch Olga position the last piece of antenna atop the CN Tower? You were? Well, sorry to be the one to break the news but you're now twenty years older.

"Tell me it's not so! There's no way! Can't be!," they all cried.

Sorry, but it's true. It was on this very day two decades ago that a Sikorsky Skycrane helicopter, the largest commercial helicopter in the world, affectionately christened Olga by her three all-male crew, gingerly positioned the final six-ton, thirty-two-foot-long section of steel antenna atop nine other pieces positioned atop the concrete structure by the giant helicopter in the interval since her arrival at the Island Airport on March 9.

Model of the CN Tower in the proposed Metro Centre setting, February 6, 1969.

The placement of this last section of antenna was the most difficult, and dangerous due to unpredictable wind gusts that managed to tear a huge Canadian flag, unfurled by steelworkers perched on the antenna when Olga's final task was completed, from the 335-foot mast. The flag's ultimate fate is still unknown. Nevertheless, the $230,000 contract with California-based Erikson Air-Crane to top off the tower utilizing Olga talents had reduced what would have been a six-month job to less than four weeks. Once the antenna was in place almost fifteen months would go by before the tower was ready to open its lofty observation decks and revolving restaurant to visitors.

The idea of a tower gracing the city skyline was first proposed in late 1968, when Canadian National and Canadian Pacific jointly announced a plan to redevelop a huge 187-acre parcel of land south of Front Street between Yonge and Bathurst streets. To be known as Metro Centre, this massive project was described by the proponents as the "most extensive and ambitious downtown redevelopment project ever undertaken in North America."

Courtesy Toronto Sun, Toronto Telegram Collection.

When Olga added this section to the CN Tower antenna on March 31, 1975, the city's newest landmark became the world's tallest free-standing structure at 1,756 feet. Two days later Olga's work was done when the final antenna segment was lowered into place, increasing the tower's height to 1,815 feet, 5 inches.

Unfortunately Olga was scrapped a few years ago. She would have made a great (and recognizable) piece of public art.

Not everyone thought the idea a good one, and when it was revealed that Union Station would be sacrificed in the name of progress opponents found a common rallying point. Nearly thirty years later the stately station still stands and the name Metro Centre now refers to the more modest development around Metro Hall at King and John streets.

A major component of the original Metro Centre complex was to be a state-of-the-art communications centre that would feature a soaring tower with a full range of broadcasting antennas and an observation deck at the 1,200-foot level. Things started to go badly for the Metro Centre advocates. Eventually, Canadian National officials decided they would pursue the communications tower idea on their own. In addition to the broadcast capabilities and the observation deck proposed for the original, though unnamed, tower, the new CN Tower, as it would be called, would also feature fine dining facilities, a lounge, snack bars, and shops in an effort to make it more of a tourist destination. The project, described as Phase I of Metro Centre, was formally announced at a press conference held on February 5, 1973. Later, during that same conference, it was boldly stated that a new Transportation Centre, south of and replacing the old Union Station, would be started later in 1973. We're still waiting for that one.

Since this column appeared I have discovered that Olga is still very much alive and is now owned by the U.S.-based Evergreen Helicopter Company and is one of that company's fleet of rotary winged aircraft. Presently, Olga is hard at work airlifting huge logs out of British Columbia forests.

PORTRAIT OF THE PAST
April 9, 1995

One of the great things about writing this column (something I started doing on a regular once-a-week basis exactly twenty years ago) is that just when you think you've seen every old Toronto photograph along comes another one, or, as happened last week, along comes another two.

The source of these photos is *Sunday Sun* reader John Vinklers, an Ontario Land Surveyor who came across them while doing some research on the life of William McIntosh, a land surveyor with the provincial Department of Mines who, it is believed, died in 1984.

The mystery is why McIntosh kept these particular photos. John thinks that McIntosh's father might be one of the individuals in these photos. Nevertheless, I certainly was grateful to get copies of the two photos and thought I'd share the old views with my readers.

• • •

The first photo shows car number 50, one of several huge electric radial cars (called radials because the routes on which they operated radiated out from the City of Toronto) operating on the Metropolitan Division of the Toronto and York Radial Railway. Initially organized in 1877 as the Metropolitan Street Railway Company of Toronto, this pioneer commuter line was established to provide service along Yonge Street between the city streetcar terminus just south of the CPR crossing near Birch Avenue and the suburban crossroads community that had grown up around the Eglinton Avenue intersection. Initial plans called for a steam operation, but that idea was rejected by township officials. Years went by and it wasn't until January 26, 1885, that the first of the horse-drawn 'Met' cars finally went into revenue service.

Over the ensuing years the "end of rail" kept advancing northward so that by the time electric vehicles were introduced in 1899 the terminus was at the entrance to the popular Glen Grove Park (now Glengrove Avenue). Three years later the terminus had been pushed north to York Mills in the hollow named for pioneer settler James Hogg.

The years went by and the big green cars moved further and further

The Standard Bank of Canada occupied the ground floor of this building which still stands at the northeast corner of Yonge Street and Erskine Avenue in north Toronto. City directories reveal the structure was erected about 1915. The Standard was established in 1873 and merged with the Bank of Commerce in 1928 for, as the papers reported, "efficiency and logic reasons." The latter bank became part of the new Canadian Imperial Bank of Commerce in 1961. Is William McIntosh's father one of the fellows in the photo?

north stirring up clouds of dust as they rumbled through Yonge Street communities like Lansing (at Sheppard Avenue), Newton Brook (at the Drewery/Cummer corner), Thornhill, Richmond Hill, and Aurora, entering the little town of Newmarket in 1899. In 1904 the operation became part of the mighty Mackenzie web of rail lines and renamed the Toronto and York Radial Railway, Metropolitan

The Standard Bank Building still stands, as seen in this May 1995 photograph.

Division (the latter part of the title to distinguish it from the radial's Scarborough and Mimico affiliates.

Radial car number 50 (seen here somewhere on Yonge Street) cost the company $8,400 in 1911. Is one of the crew William McIntosh's father?

In 1907 Metropolitan Division cars were running into Jackson's Point on Lake Simcoe and two years later into Sutton. Operation of the forty-eight-mile-long line was assumed by the TTC in early 1927 only to be abandoned on March 16, 1930. Then, just four months later, service was reinstated as far north as Richmond Hill. Due in part to the serious electrical power shortage throughout the province following the end of the war, service on what had become known as the North Yonge Railways was curtailed once and for all on October 10, 1948.

Radial car 50, described in the official record book as a double-truck, double-end motor passenger car with seating for forty and powered by four GE 40-horsepower motors, was built in 1911 in Preston, Ontario.

Following the appearance of this column, a reader informed me that William McIntosh's father, John James McIntosh, was the Town of North Toronto's police chief in 1911 (often seen on patrol with his horse, Victor) and when that community was annexed by the City of Toronto in 1912 McIntosh, not Victor, was taken on strength by the city force. He was also a house-painter, thus accounting for his presence (whichever one he is) with the group of painters in front of the Standard Bank.

AND NOW THE NEWS
April 16, 1995

John Ross Robertson, founder of the *Toronto Telegram.*

Many readers of the *Toronto Sun* are aware that this paper was born just hours after the *Toronto Telegram* presses were shut down for the last time on October 30, 1971. The *Tely* (as most people called the popular paper) was born on April 18, 1876, exactly 119 years ago next Tuesday, as *The Evening Telegram* and was the creation of businessman and philanthropist John Ross Robertson. The *Telegram*'s near century-long history is told in the late Ron Poulton's fascinating 1971 publication *The Paper Tyrant.*

When several former *Telegram* employees indicated that they were going to bring out a new paper John Bassett, owner of the *Telegram*, gave them a complete run of the paper on dozens and dozens of rolls of microfilm and while the good old *Tely* hasn't been published now for nearly a quarter of a century, its stories and columns continue to be a great source material for my *Sunday Sun* columns.

I'm especially intrigued by stories from years gone by that have a present-day connection.

Take the following stories, for instance (with the date they originally ran in the *Telegram* in brackets):

One of the pupils of the George Street school was yesterday expelled by the headmaster for carrying a loaded revolver around in his pocket. This is a common practice with the youth of this city.

(March 12, 1878)

The increased cost of living has been heard from again. This time Toronto hospitals have spoken. Some months ago they got legislation passed enabling them to increase public ward charges and this morning representatives of Grace, St. Michael's, Western and General Hospitals appeared before the elected officials at City Hall with a request that the civic per diem allowance be increased. It was reported that the 4 hospitals are losing $19,000 annually.

(May 25, 1904)

As the roads in the vicinity of Toronto are said to be among the worst in Canada the Toronto Automobile Club has started a movement to have them improved. Accordingly the club has decided to offer at least $300 to municipalities for road improving competitions. There will be 3 prizes, $550, $200 and $100 respectively which will be paid to the municipalities which show the piece of roadway 1 mile long on which the greatest improvement has been made.

(September 11, 1906)

An innovation with regard to police control of street traffic will commence Monday morning when a force of 10 policemen will be assigned special bicycle duty for the regulation of vehicle traffic.

(July 24, 1909)

Robertson was also responsible for the establishment of the Hospital for Sick Children. The photo shows the facility on College Street prior to its move to its present building at 555 University Avenue. This building is now occupied by the Toronto Branch of the Canadian Red Cross.

It was announced in Ottawa today that gasoline prices are to be investigated by the select committee on banking and commerce. MP Thomas Donnelly of Willow Bunch, in presenting his motion, argued there was no justification for Canadian gasoline being higher in price than gasoline sold in American cities. The average price in American cities last year was 15 cents per gallon while in Canadian cities the average was 23 cents.

(February 12, 1932)

An all-out drive to curb the crime wave sweeping across Toronto and large Ontario cities has been launched by the mayor and a thorough investigation is being conducted by city police commissioners and police officials into reports that "hot guns and automatics" are being sold on the underworld market for as low as $20. The crime wave has reached alarming proportions. Within the past 3 weeks there has been an average of 2 hold-ups per day and shop-breaking and safecracking is being carried out on a large scale. Within the past 3 days there have been a half dozen hold-ups in this city. "Toronto has always had the reputation of being a law-abiding city but frankly I am perturbed at the unusual wave of crime which has swept through in recent weeks," said the mayor.

(September 5, 1945)

In the not too distant future motorists in Toronto, Oshawa, Beaverton, Penetang, Brampton and Burlington areas will be able to lift a telephone from a hook in their own car and receive and send messages.

(September 12, 1949)

Ever since President Kennedy was killed with a mail order rifle that anyone could purchase for less than $14 there has been a great deal of talk about curbing the sale and use of guns of all types. But the misuse of guns has been like the weather – everybody talking about it and nobody doing anything about it. It is common among the sporting set to argue that nothing should be done beyond education, but it would make as much sense to argue that education alone can solve the traffic safety problem. Why should not registration be required for all guns, at the very least?

(March 10, 1964)

GOLDEN OLDIES
April 23, 1995

I t was my good fortune to attend the recent second anniversary performance of *Forever Plaid* at the New Yorker Theatre. After more than 700 performances the cast was as fresh and spontaneous as they were opening night. For those who have yet to see the production the story revolves around four young singers who, having been wiped out in a traffic accident on February 9, 1964, while on their way to the quartet's first major 'gig,' are given a second chance and return to earth to give the performance of their (reprieved) lives.

While *Forever Plaid* was born off-Broadway in 1990 (and didn't make it to Toronto for another three years), the production has more of a Canadian connection

Casino Theatre on Queen Street West was once the hotspot of Toronto entertainment. It opened in 1936 and was demolished in 1965.

than one would first expect. For instance, one of the songs featured in the show, *Crazy 'Bout Ya Baby*, was made popular by a Toronto foursome, the Crew Cuts. This group was a product of St. Michael's Cathedral Choir School and known originally as the Four Tones. The fellows renamed themselves the Canadaires and were discovered while performing in Cleveland, Ohio. Following a third name change the boys recorded "Crazy 'Bout Ya Baby" for the influential Mercury Records organization in early 1954. This song was big on the hit parade about the same time Toronto's Yonge Street subway opened. Their biggest hit, a song with the unforgettable title "Sh-Boom," made the charts a few months later.

Two other songs in the show "Moments to Remember" and "No, Not Much" were huge hits in 1955 and 1956, respectively, for a second Toronto-born quartet, the Four Lads. The group was another product of St. Michael's

Cathedral Choir School, though the Lads predated the Crew Cuts by a few years, having made their public debut in 1949 on CBC Radio's "Canadian Cavalcade," an immensely popular program hosted by the late Elwood Glover.

A fourth song in *Forever Plaid* also has an interesting 'Toronto-connection.' When American-born singer Johnnie Ray decided to record "Cry" in 1951 as a follow-up record to his highly successful "Little White Cloud that Cried," both he and arranger Mitch Miller selected a quartet made up of four young men from Toronto to sing background. The group was the up-and-coming Four Lads.

Early the following year Johnnie Ray arrived in Toronto where he was to be the headline act at the Casino Theatre, an extremely popular city playhouse located on the south side of Queen Street West (between Bay and York streets) approximately where the main entrance to the Sheraton Centre is today.

Johnnie Ray (arrow) signs autographs for his adoring audience at the Casino's stage door.

In the years that followed the opening of Lou Appelby's new theatre in 1936 the place became home to virtually every kind of performance allowed by law (and some that weren't), including burlesque, vaudeville, 'off-Broadway'-type plays, motion pictures, and 'big-name' performers. Falling into this latter classification were people like Henny Youngman, Phil Silvers, Victor Borge, Mickey Rooney, Basil Rathbone (performing Shakespeare), Tex Ritter, Louie Armstrong, Tommy Dorsey, the Mills Brothers, the Andrew Sisters, Eartha Kitt, Rosemary Clooney, and in 1952 for a five-day stint from February 21 through to the 27th (but never on Sunday), one of the top crooners of the day, Johnnie Ray. With him for that date were Toronto's Four Lads who were just starting to be noticed, though still several years away from going out on their own. Others on the bill were child acrobats Nina & Pepi, an act called Adrian & Charlie (doing 'bumps and bounces') while the film *Joe Palooka in the Squared Circle* was on screen.

Ray's five-day stint broke all house attendance records and in appreciation manager Murray Little increased the performer's agreed-upon weekly remuneration from $400 to $4000. There's no indication in those same newspaper accounts as to what the Lads were getting. Their time was still to come.

THE LAST VOYAGE
April 30, 1995

Eighty years ago today on April 30, 1915, hundreds of people from all over the continent were converging on the bustling City of New York. Early the next morning they would make their way to Pier 54 at the foot of Fourteenth Street where the magnificent Cunard transatlantic ocean liner *Lusitania* was berthed. Of the 1,959 passengers scheduled to cross on the luxury liner, a total of 322 were citizens of the Dominion of Canada; of that number nearly half were from Toronto.

The decision to build the mighty *Lusitania* and her sister, *Mauretania*, was as a result of Great Britain's desire to win back the coveted Blue Riband, the pennant flown with pride by the fastest vessel on the North Atlantic run. At the start of 1915 the Blue Riband was held by a German liner. With the First World War almost a year old, reclaiming that pennant would do wonders to boost England's sagging morale.

To ensure that the new Cunard liners would indeed be the fastest on the Atlantic it was determined that each new craft would be powered by four immense steam turbines, a radical departure from the more usual recip-rocating-type steam engine. The turbines were designed to give each liner a top speed of twenty-six knots, more than enough to capture the Riband and outrun any enemy submarine.

It was obvious that to build and furnish these leviathans, more money than Cunard dared to put up would be needed. The importance of these vessels to the country's future was so great that the British government advanced Cunard more than £2 million and agreed to provide an annual subsidy of £150,000 on condition that the government would have a claim on the ships in the event of a national emergency. No doubt this use could include the carrying of munitions. But whether *Lusitania* did or did not during her May 1915 crossing is still the subject of debate.

Since the outbreak of war on August 4, 1914, *Lusitania* had made a half-dozen transatlantic round-trips, and even though the shutting down of six of her twenty-three massive boilers to conserve coal had reduced her speed significantly each crossing went by without incident.

Therefore there seemed little chance that the May sailing would be any different, even though an advertisement placed by German authorities in a few American newspapers cautioning travellers against selecting British

Penny postcard of the ill-fated _Lusitania_.

ships or those of her allies did give some passengers cause for concern. A very few passengers did, in fact, change bookings. Some even canceled their trip. But for most, _Lusitania's_ exemplary safety record guaranteed a safe crossing.

Amongst the hundreds of passengers excitedly waving farewell as _Lusitania_ backed away from her Pier 54 berth were 155 Torontonians, including such local notables as Reliable Knitting Company's president George Copping and his wife, Frank Rogers, one of Simpson's most promising young managers who was accompanied by his bride of less than a week, Alfred Clarke, founder of the A.R. Clarke Leather Company on Eastern Avenue (when it was announced that the vessel was attacked by a German ship the company immediately fired all its German employees), Mrs. G. Sterling Ryerson, wife of the Commissioner of the Dominion Red Cross who was traveling to England to comfort her young son Lieutenant Arthur Ryerson who had been wounded in action (and died soon after the sinking), James Rogers, publisher of the weekly newspaper _Jack Canuck_, and Sir John Eaton's niece Iris Burnside. Interestingly, Sir John had been on _Lusitania's_ 1907 maiden voyage. Also on board were four managers from Eaton's downtown Toronto store.

The crossing was uneventful. Then, at a few minutes after 2:00 PM on May 7 as _Lusitania_ cruised ten miles south of the Irish coastline, a white streak appeared off starboard side of the ship. Seconds later there was a deafening explosion. The torpedo fired by the UC-97's Kapitänleutanant Walther Schwieger had found its mark.

The first explosion was followed almost immediately by a second and the mighty ship began to take on a sickening list. Passengers and crew alike scrambled as cold green ocean water poured into the vessel. Just eighteen minutes after the initial blast the 31,500-ton, 790-foot-long *Lusitania* was no more. With her went the hopes and dreams of 1,195 passengers and crew. Included in that number were 175 Canadians, eighty-two of whom would never return to families and loved ones here in Toronto.

In addition to the social luminaries listed above, the indifferent Atlantic Ocean claimed hard-working, God-fearing Albert Palmer, his wife and their three young children who lived in a small house at 79 Vermont Avenue near Bathurst and Dupont.

Close-up of the Clarke gravestone in Mt. Pleasant Cemetery.

V-E DAY PLUS FIFTY
May 7, 1995

Fifty years ago today on May 7, 1945, pandemonium reigned in the City of Toronto. The war in Europe was finally over!!

Actually, the day had dawned much like any other had ever since the Allies (including the Canadian 3rd Division) had stormed the Normandy beaches the previous June 6 to initiate the liberation of Europe. But in recent days rumours had kept cropping up that the Germans were on the verge of giving it all up. Nothing official mind you, but all of those rumors must have some substance behind them.

Celebrations on Bay Street, V-E Day 1945.

Shortly after nine on that Monday morning an unexplainable feeling of excitement could be felt coursing through the city's downtown core. Actually, the most obvious change in the day-to-day activities was the presence of more than the normal number of policemen taking up positions at busy intersections and on street patrol. Chief of Police Draper was taking no chances. Should those rumours, now more

PROCLAMATION!
PUBLIC HOLIDAY
AS ALREADY ANNOUNCED
MAY 8th, 1945
Will be a Public Holiday in observance of
V-E DAY
ROBERT H. SAUNDERS, K.C.,
Mayor
GOD SAVE THE KING!

The public proclamation that appeared in daily newspapers on May 7, 1945.

prevalent than ever, come true, his men would be ready.

Then, suddenly, just as the bells of the City Hall clock finished chiming the half-hour, the air was filled with cheering voices. It was true; the war with Germany was over.

Though the unconditional surrender had taken place at Reims in France on May 7 at 0:41 AM (Greenwich Mean time) with the surrender terms to become effective at 10:31 that night (GMT), the major powers had agreed that the official announcement would be made simultaneously by Churchill, Truman, and Stalin. The British and American leaders were ready to make their announcements on the seventh, but the Russian leader wasn't. It was decided, therefore, to declare the next day, May 8, Victory in Europe Day.

Attempts were made by officials to downplay news of the May 7 signing, but those attempts were to no avail. The world had been waiting too long! Let the celebrations begin!!

Here in Toronto the rest of May 7 was devoted to spontaneous parades, street dances ("Pistol Packin' Mama, Put That Pistol Down" seemed to be the favourite tune), smooching with strangers, horn blowing – you name it. Whatever it was, it was okay that day.

Up at the RCAF's number 1 Initial Training School (before the war it was the Eglinton Hunt Club), the carved caricatures of Hitler and Hirohito above the station's Victory Loan campaign poster were smashed to pieces, while the effigies of Mussolini and Herr Hitler suspended from the hydro wires on Gerrard Street, just east of Broadview, made a spectacular fire later in the evening. At the Danforth and Langford intersection another Hirohito effigy wearing a sign reading "SO SORRY, YOU'RE NEXT" was soon an unrecognizable lump of rags and cardboard.

Downtown, as horns honked and streetcar gongs gonged (it was all in good fun, no-one was going anywhere quickly), the main streets were overflowing with people and littered with ticker tape. The presence of the latter seemed particularly unusual since in a week's time the National Salvage Committee would be holding a massive waste paper drive. Well, at least the Works people knew where they could get a lot of it easily.

The Toronto Stock Exchange opened as usual but the public's unprecedented run on the phone system forced the Exchange to close just thirty minutes after opening.

In the skies overhead Toronto-built Mosquito fighters and Lancaster bombers buzzed back and forth adding their distinctive sounds to the joyous cacophony.

As the night wore on many suddenly realized thousands who had gone to war would never return. The raucous celebrations soon gave way to an air of solemnity. May 8, the official V-E Day, was declared a national public holiday. In Toronto much of the day would be devoted to church services, both of the open-air variety at City Hall and in Riverdale Park and in neighbourhood houses of worship. In Scarborough crowds gathered at the recently erected Victory Bowl at Birchmount and Kingston roads. In Oakville services were held in the town's Victoria Park, while up in Weston citizens quietly paraded from Memorial School to the Town Hall where Mayor Jack Allan addressed the solemn crowd. In Swansea hundreds gathered in front of the Veterans' Hall at Durie and Deforest streets before parading to Rennie Park.

On Wednesday it was time to get back to work. The world was still at war with Japan.

OPEN THE GATES
May 14, 1995

O ver the years stories that start off with few, if any, elements of truth tend to become unquestioned facts. Take, for instance, the story about the distinctive gates that are part of the wrought-iron fence that surrounds Osgoode Hall on Queen Street at University. Most people continue to assume that the gates were constructed as cattle gates to keep local bovines off the Hall's lush lawn and away from the appetizing flower beds. The intricately designed entrance structures require that all visitors (two or four-legged) first enter the gate, immediately change direction, navigate through an eighteen-inch-wide opening, then change direction once more before finally being clear of the fence. To be sure, a cow cannot carry out the manoeuvre just described. This fact was proven unequivocally during a media stunt performed back in 1950.

However, what really makes the cattle gate theory suspect is the fact that when the present fence and gates were erected in the mid-1860s the closest herd had an appointment at the market a mile or so to the east.

That's not to say that at some point in the Hall's history there wouldn't have been cattle in the vicinity. In Patrick Slater's book, *The Yellow Briar*, Jack Trueman's cattle are described as having "a headstrong notion that their path should lead across the field in front of Osgoode Hall." While it's true young Jack kept two cows in a small barn behind his father's Tavern Tyrone,

Looking north on York Street to Osgoode Hall, October 1923.

a popular watering hole that stood where 'old' City Hall stands today, closer investigation reveals that the Slater was describing our city in 1847, almost four decades before the fence and gates around Osgoode Hall were ordered built.

Same view, March 1995.

In a publication put out by the Law Society of Upper Canada, the organization that commissioned the building of the first section of Osgoode Hall in 1829 (and suggested it be named in honour of the province's first Chief Justice William Osgoode who never did visit our community during his 1792–94 term) suggests that the fence and gates were actually erected as a defensive measure. This makes perfect sense since the American Civil War was just ending and many feared that next on the Union army's agenda was the invasion of British North America. At least the gates would slow up those rifle-totting Yankees so that the defenders of the province's judicial headquarters could "pick them off." The attempted invasion of Canada by the Fenian Brotherhood in 1866 only strengthened the resolve of the Osgoode Hall patrol to be on guard.

One other reason for the inhibiting gates has been postulated. At the time the gates and fence were erected (a $20,000 project carried out by the St. Lawrence Foundry) several streets to the west of Osgoode Hall were lined with the residences of many wealthy families, most of whom employed a nanny to look after the children. It has been suggested that the narrow gates were, in fact, installed to keep the nannies from wheeling the perambulators onto the Hall's lawns whilst "chatting up" the lawyers.

• • •

Tom Brooks of Gravenhurst, Ontario, has just self-published a new book on the American Civil War and, unlike others written on this fascinating subject, Tom's has Canadian content. Nine members of the famous 10th Louisiana Infantry were Canadian, one of whom, young Jerry Cronan, holds the distinction of being one of 482 members of the Confederate Army buried in Arlington National Cemetery and the only Canadian. In addition to the Canadians the 10th boasted men from twenty-two different countries. *Lee's Foreign Legion* (softcover, 280 pages, maps, photos, $28.45, including postage, with cheque or money order payable to T.W. Brooks) is available from Tom at 139 Pratt Street, Gravenhurst, Ontario P1P 1P5.

ON THE WATERFRONT
May 21, 1995

Several weeks ago I wrote about the removal of the York Street underpass, that long, dark, passageway south of Front Street that, ever since its completion in 1930, has been both a physical and psychological obstacle hindering the public's access to Toronto's waterfront. That obstruction is no more. Now we have to work on those darn underpasses on Yonge and Bay streets.

One easy way to demonstrate the remarkable changes that have occurred along Toronto's waterfront over the years is through the use of old and contemporary photographs taken from similar vantage points. For instance, almost eight decades separate the photos accompanying this column. In the centre of the earlier view we see the Toronto Harbour Commission Building nearing completion in 1918. Built on the edge of Toronto Bay to demonstrate the newly formed Toronto Harbour Commissioners' faith in the future of the city's waterfront, the $245,000 structure was designed by the prominent Canadian architectural firm of Chapman and McGiffin. Other fine examples of Alfred Chapman's work can be seen in the Princes' Gate, the former Ontario Government Building in Exhibition Park, and the former Crosse and Blackwell Building (now MTV) at the southeast corner of Lake Shore Boulevard and Bathurst Street.

The city's waterfront in 1918. Under construction is the Toronto Harbour Commission Building, number two in the contemporary view.

Toronto's waterfront area today.

Also visible in the view is the lake steamer SS *Kingston* moored just south of the old York Street temporary bridge. This 855-passenger side-wheeler was built in 1901 at the Bertram shipyard that was situated on the water's edge east of the old Western Channel. Years later massive landfilling operations would cover the channel (a new, safer entrance was built further to the south) and today's busy Bathurst Street/Lake Shore Boulevard intersection covers the site. SS *Kingston* operated for many years on the popular Toronto–Rochester–Prescott route until the vessel was retired in 1949 and subsequently scrapped.

The contemporary view, taken this past February, shows the view from the garage south of the Metro Toronto Convention Centre on Front Street. Painfully visible are the railway tracks that continue to cut the city off from its waterfront. The glass-walled structure is SkyWalk connecting Union Station with the CN Tower and SkyDome. Beyond the walkway are:

1) The Postal Delivery Building (proposed new home of the Raptors basketball team) at 40 Bay Street at the corner of Lake Shore Boulevard West,
2) Toronto Harbour Commission Building (still under construction in the 1918 photo),
3) WaterPark Place (Bay Street and Queen's Quay),
4) Harbour Square, and
5) Harbour Side condominium towers on Queen's Quay West,
6) SkyWalk,
7) One York Quay condominium towers at the foot of York Street.

"BRIDGES OF YORK COUNTY"
May 28, 1995

A week or so ago Metro Toronto's newest bridge was officially opened. Located at the mouth of the Humber River the structure is unlike any other bridge in at least two respects. First, the new structure is restricted to pedestrian and bicycle traffic only – no cars or trucks. And second, it's pretty to look at, an unusual characteristic for something that's usually strictly utilitarian. The Humber River Bicycle-Pedestrian Bridge, to give the 139-meter-long structure its formal title, was budgeted at just over $4 million with funds coming from the province, Metro, the cities of Etobicoke and Toronto, and the Waterfront Regeneration Trust. The latter organization has a special interest in the new bridge in that the structure forms a connecting link between the aforementioned cities on the Trust's new 325-kilometer-long Waterfront Trail. Original plans had pedestrian and bicycle traffic crossing the Humber River via a sidewalk incorporated into one of six new vehicle bridges scheduled to be built over the river in the next seven or eight years. However, in an unusually bold and sensitive move, officials decided instead

Lakeshore Road bridge at the Humber River, 1883.

to erect a bridge solely for the use of pedestrians and cyclists. To ensure that this new structure would be a fitting landmark at the mouth of this historic watercourse (in the early days referred to as the Toronto Passage), architects, landscapers, and artists joined with a structural design team to create Metro's newest and most imaginative bridge.

• • •

The new Humber River Bicycle-Pedestrian Bridge is the most recent in a long list of structures, large and small, to span the lower Humber River. It would appear that the first, a simple wooden structure, was erected sometime in the late 1700s over the river that was then simply referred to as the St. John River in recognition of a pioneer settler living on

New Humber River bicycle-pedestrian bridge, officially opened May 16, 1995.

its banks. A few more years were to go by before the term Humber was first applied to the watercourse. That name was selected by Elizabeth Simcoe, wife of the governor, soon after the couple's arrival in the early 1790s. Elizabeth selected the name (and that of the Don) after rivers she was familiar with in the northeast of England.

As York County's earliest records were destroyed by fire, the early history of the lower Humber is sketchy at best. Nevertheless, a map drawn in 1838 shows a more substantial structure that also appears on an 1854 map along with a second structure a little closer to the lakeshore. Both bridges were constructed to convey both pedestrian and horse- and ox-drawn traffic traveling a very rudimentary, and dusty, lakeshore road over the river.

Some history books refer to a swing bridge being erected in the early 1840s, though specific features of this structure have yet to be found. It is known that a flood in 1850 carried the bridge into the lake.

The first major structure to span the river appeared in 1866. It, too, was made of wood though longer (at three spans) and wider than the others to handle the ever-increasing traffic traveling along the lakeshore to and from the growing City of Toronto.

While these first few bridges were designed to convey only pedestrian and light carts and wagons over the river, the arrival of the steam railways on the scene meant that heavier bridges would be necessary. The first of these, though still of wood construction, was erected in 1866 when the tracks of the Great Western Railway were laid between Toronto and Hamilton. Then as railway equipment increased in size and weight so, too, did the bridge structures. In 1888 an iron bridge was built and an addition was erected four years later to permit the line to be double-tracked. Over the following years newer and larger railway bridges were erected to handle new and larger locomotives and rolling stock. In 1916, a bridge of the Warren truss variety, that had been erected in 1903 and was now too light for continued railway service, was dismantled, moved to what was then the foot of Bathurst Street, and re-erected. Today the recycled Humber railway bridge is still in use carrying streetcar, pedestrian, and vehicular traffic over the railway corridor south of Front Street.

Vehicle bridges at the mouth of the Humber also continued to evolve with a new steel truss structure erected in 1900. The present bridges were built in 1930. They suffered major damage in October of 1954 when Hurricane Hazel's flood waters tore out the west approaches. These structures are due for replacement over the next few years.

DOME TURNS SIX
June 4, 1995

I t hardly seems possible, but it was exactly six years ago yesterday, June 3, 1989, that Toronto's marvelous new SkyDome was officially opened in the pouring rain. Perhaps you were one of the several hundred attendees that night who, in addition to witnessing the spectacular inaugural ceremony, went home with a special souvenir, soggy wet clothing, as a result of Chuck Magwood's decision to open the revolutionary retractable roof in spite of the dismal weather outside. There's little doubt that had officials not opened the roof certain members of the media plus a handful of perpetual nay-sayers would have quickly crowed that the Canadian-designed and -built, one of a kind, fully retractable roof didn't work after all. Canadians, for some unfathomable reason, are like that.

The only sour note during the Dome's opening week was the fact that the Blue Jays lost their very first home game in the place against Milwaukee. How good's your memory? Who threw the Jay's first pitch, was it a strike or a ball, and what was the final score of that historic first game? See the end of this column for answers to these three questions and details about a very special prize awaiting a reader who can correctly answer a fourth.

Now that six years have gone by since SkyDome opened it has, like the CN Tower (twenty years old next year), City Hall (thirty in September), and a host of other city landmarks, become just another city building to most of us locals. And while I still find the opening and closing of the 8,700-ton trio of roof panels fascinating to watch, most of the "ooing and ahhing" is now done by visitors to our great city.

With SkyDome now a permanent fixture on Toronto's skyline, it's interesting to look back on what might have been had initial ideas about the location of Toronto's new sports facility been accepted. For instance, instead of heading for the waterfront fans might have been making tracks for Downsview Airport, a location proffered by perpetual North York Mayor Mel Lastman. However, test flights directly over the heads of 50,000 spectators in the dome by aircraft built in the nearby de Havilland factory was considered both unwise and potentially unhealthy.

Another possibility was a site in north Etobicoke near the Woodbine race track but the lack of an existing mass transit link doomed this plan from the start. The third possibility was the construction of a new stadium

Artist's concept of Jack Allan's 1960 stadium proposal to be built just east of the CP roundhouse. SkyDome would be built just west of the roundhouse and opened twenty-five years after this sketch was made. Note the proposed Raptor home, Postal Delivery Building at the Lake Shore Boulevard and Bay Street intersection (see arrow).

The John B. Parkin Associates 1969 North York stadium proposal. Note Allen Road and Downsview Airport runways.

at Exhibition Place replacing the venerable old grandstand. Interestingly, this particular location had been promoted for decades as the obvious site of a new so-called civic stadium. In a July 28, 1953 newspaper article the lead story is headlined:

PLAN STADIUM FOR 60,000

The story goes on to announce that plans were under way to build a 60,000-seat stadium at the Exhibition to back Toronto's bid for either the 1960 or 1964 Olympic Games. Actually they were simply going to add 36,000 seats to the existing 24,000 seats under the covered stands creating a massive bowl-shaped facility. The cost of the revamped structure (in 1953) was to be a mere $2 million.

As the search for a site of the new stadium progressed each of the aforementioned locations was dismissed. Then in 1985 a new location entered the picture. This one was at the foot of John Street on a parcel described as being part of the railway lands. At first it appeared that the choice of this site was entirely original. However, a search of the history books revealed that in fact East York Reeve Jack Allan had promoted a location a few hundred feet to the east a quarter of century earlier!

Work on the new 60,000-seat, retractable roof (a feature of the new facility that came as a real surprise when announced) officially began at a ground-breaking ceremony held on October 3, 1986. Exactly 974 days later Canada's spectacular new SkyDome welcomed its first guests.

• • •

Here are the answers to the SkyDome opening ball game mini-test: Jimmy Key, fastball strike, 5 to 3.

Now, for the special quiz. The first response selected from all entries correctly answering the question, "Name the Canadian who designed SkyDome's retractable roof?" (and no it wasn't architect Rod Robbie, so save your stamp) will receive, thanks to SkyDome's David Garrick, a pair of tickets to watch a Blue Jay game from one of the magnificent Skyboxes, a personal tour of SkyDome with David, and the once-in-a-lifetime opportunity to push the button that opens good old what's his name's revolutionary retractable roof. A photo of the winner pushing the button and a special certificate recognizing the occasion will also be presented. The winner will be selected from all entries received up to and including June 16, 1995. Send your answer to SKYDOME'S 6TH, c/o "The Way We Were," Toronto *Sunday Sun*, 333 King Street East, Toronto M5A 3X5.

A LITTLE EX-TRA TRAVEL
June 11, 1995

Visitors to Toronto's annual Canadian National Exhibition have relied on public transportation to and from the grounds almost since the fair's inception in 1879. And since 1916 a major component of that service has been provided by streetcars operating to the loop at the east end of the grounds.

Now, as a result of the imminent start of construction of the mammoth new National Trade Centre south of the Coliseum and Industry Building, that loop will officially close next Saturday. As a result, for the first time in more than seventy-five years, there will be no streetcar service to the east end of the CNE this year. Instead a TTC bus service will operate on the *Bathurst* route from the subway to a loop located between the Automotive Building and Marine Museum.

Two years from now streetcars will return to the Ex, but, it is planned, will operate along Manitoba Drive (north of the Coliseum) to the GO Transit station, a routing that was first proposed in 1930. That's why the north façade, originally to be the main entranceway to the building, is much more impressive than that on the south. In fact, the south side had to be given an improvised main entrance when the idea of having the streetcars serve the north entrance was abandoned.

• • •

It was during the 1881 Toronto Industrial Exhibition that public transit first became an integral part of what has become, under the name Canadian National Exhibition, one of the world's largest annual fairs. During that year's Ex horse-drawn streetcars of the Toronto Street Railway operating on the King line were routed down Strachan Avenue to Wellington Street. From there it was just a short walk to the hustle and bustle of the Exhibition grounds.

The King line was electrified on September 5, 1892, and during the run of the fair the new-fangled electric cars were routed down Dufferin Street to loop at Springhurst Avenue opposite the old west entrance to the grounds that back then was located on the east side of Dufferin.

It wasn't until 1906 that the city acquired forty acres of property west of

Manitoba Drive and the north façade of the Coliseum, once the proposed main entrance to a building that in its day had the greatest area under one roof in the world. The planned realignment of the Bathurst car line will approximate a 1930 routing proposal.

Courtesy TTC Archives.

TTC east entrance loop, in use for decades, closed in mid-1995.

Dufferin Street and the present layout of the west end of the grounds began to take shape.

In an effort to entice visitors to the less populated east end of the grounds an attempt was made in 1905 to run a service to that part of the property. To get the Bathurst cars to the new loop it would have been necessary to lay tracks right through the middle of Fort York. Members of the Ontario Historical Society and the Old Fort Protective Association fought the idea warning that the ill-conceived plan would destroy the integrity of the historic site.

As a result of this confrontation, the eagerly sought after streetcar service to the east end of the CNE didn't materialize until August 25, 1916.

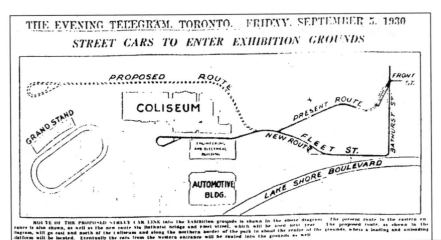

STREET CARS TO ENTER EXHIBITION GROUNDS

ROUTE OF THE PROPOSED STREET CAR LINE into the Exhibition grounds is shown in the above diagram. The present route to the eastern entrance is also shown, as well as the new route via Bathurst bridge and Fleet street, which will be used next year. The proposed route, as shown in the diagram, will go east and north of the Coliseum and along the northern border of the park to about the centre of the grounds, where a loading and unloading platform will be located. Eventually the cars from the western entrance will be routed into the grounds as well

The new route for streetcars entering the east end of the CNE grounds is similar to that proposed in 1930, as shown in this *Evening Telegram* map. Today's GO station is near the west loop in the sketch.

On that day Bathurst streetcars began operating south of Front across a structure that had formerly been a steam railway bridge across the Humber River. The bridge had been disassembled and re-erected at a northeast/southwest angle at the foot of Bathurst Street. After crossing the recycled bridge the cars veered westerly and skirted the Fort's north rampart and on to the CNE's new eastern entrance.

In 1931, the old bridge was realigned in a north/south direction, track extended south to the new Fleet Street, then west to the CNE loop that'll close next Saturday.

Just days after the loop closed, it began to vanish.

ALL ABOARD FOR THE ISLAND
June 18, 1995

I t was on this very day, precisely eighty-five years ago (although June 18, 1910, was in fact a Saturday), that the newest vessel to join the lengthy list of Toronto Island ferry boats slipped into the stagnant water in the slip adjacent to the busy Polson Iron Works shipyard at the foot of Sherbourne Street. Built for the Toronto Ferry Company, a privately owned enterprise that had been granted a monopoly in 1890 by the city to provide cross-bay service, the still unnamed craft was the finest, most modern that money (well, at least $75,000 worth) could buy. It was double-ended (to serve the mainland and busy Hanlan's Point dock), had a double-compound steam engine connected to twin side-paddles, and could race across the bay at a top speed of 10 MPH.

Crowds begin to gather at the old Island ferry terminal (between Bay and York streets) as game time at the Hanlan's Point Stadium approaches. While all-day parking may have gone up to a quarter in 1923, the streetcar fare was still just seven cents.

The double-ended feature was important because the vessel would spend most of its time during the spring, summer, and fall ferrying thousands of baseball fans to and from the large stadium at Hanlan's Point to watch their beloved Maple Leafs challenge other members of the International League, an association of baseball teams one level below the majors. Being double-ended meant the craft could load and unload at both ends without having to turn the vessel in mid-bay, a manoeuvre that delayed the service.

Actually, the necessity of a new boat became apparent not long after the company put *Blue Bell*, anther double-ender, on the Hanlan's Point run in 1906. As the team became more and more popular (the team won the League championship in 1907), the cross-bay traffic increased and this, combined with a new 18,000-seat concrete stadium built to replace the antiquated wooden stand destroyed by fire on August 10, 1909, resulted in the company placing an order for a new boat with Polsons.

Though eventually christened *Trillium*, that title certainly wasn't the company's first choice. To be sure the company wanted to maintain the long-standing tradition of naming their craft after flowers (Mayflower, Primrose, Blue Bell). In fact, the first thought was to name her Arbutus (a species of evergreen), but unfortunately (or, in retrospect, fortunately) that name was already being used by some craft, somewhere, and so another choice was put forward. This time it was Hawthorne, but again the name

The parking rates may have changed, as have transit fares, but the good old *Trillium* is still around.

was in use. Then came Golden Rod. Sorry. Try again. Finally, and perhaps out of desperation, Trillium was put forward and, after a thorough search through the registry books, accepted.

And thus it was when the still-unfinished hull and superstructure slid sideways into the Polson slip eighty-five years ago today, the sturdy craft finally had a name. Two weeks later the sturdy craft, now fitted out and with the name *Trillium* proudly emblazoned on her twin paddle boxes, entered service on Toronto Bay.

In 1974–75 the vessel underwent a $1 million restoration/refurbishment program and was returned to service, the pride of the Toronto Island ferry fleet.

• • •

I've just come across a couple of dandy books that will certainly appeal to car buffs in the audience (or dads who would have rather had a book than another tie). The first, authored by former Torontonian Bill Vance, is titled *Reflections on Automotive History* and is a compilation of many of Bill's syndicated newspaper columns in which he describes the history of specific automobile models. The book is available at $18.50 (paper) or $28.50 (cloth) from Eramosa Valley Publishing, Box 370, Rockwood, Ontario N0B 2K0 (519) 856-1065.

The second book, *Old Auto Tales,* by Gord Hazlett, is a collection of whimsical, sometimes hilarious stories gleaned from this long-time East Yorker's love affair with anything to do with old cars. Available for $22.50 (tax and GST included) from the author, c/o 264 Linsmore Crescent, Toronto M4V 4L7.

This afternoon Black Creek Pioneer Village will present *A Day in the Life of a Soldier* with re-enactment groups recreating the trials and tribulations of military life during the Revolutionary War era.

The Halton County Radial Railway Museum near Rockwood, Ontario, will have many of their old streetcars out and running during its Summer extravaganza on June 25 from 10:00 AM to 5:00 PM. The museum is located eight miles north of Highway 401 at exit 38.

Interested in the future of the proposed Roundhouse Park and the old CPR roundhouse just east of SkyDome? On June 20, from noon until 6:30 PM, there'll be an open house in the main-floor lobby of City Hall at which time preliminary plans and proposals for the site will be on view and members of the park design team will be present to answer questions and listen to ideas. For further information call (416) 392-1885.

THE WILD BLUE 1950s
June 25, 1995

Wen I was a kid, one of my favourite day trips was getting together with a couple of friends and riding our bikes all the way out to the old Malton Airport (for those readers who weren't fortunate enough to grow up in Toronto or for those just too young to remember when we even had a place called Malton, that airport today is the Lester B. Pearson International Airport). And when we got there we'd hide the bikes and then pay a dime to pass through the turnstiles so we could go up on the roof of the sleek, sprawling (or so we kids thought), two-storey terminal (which served as the administration building and as the location of the control tower) and watch the airplanes come and go.

TCA Super Constellation over the Toronto waterfront in 1958, four years after the plane's introduction into service. Back then the tourist-class round-trip fare, $482.40, Montreal to Glasgow, wasn't much more than economy today.

Philip Yull's planned Mississauga Terminal Four convention/museum complex incorporating TCA Super Constellation CF-TGE.

Unlike today, when virtually everything seen at Pearson is a jet of some sort and, except for the number of engines, look pretty much alike (to be sure an occasional Dash-8 glides by), back then there were piston-engine planes of all shapes and sizes. As we peered at them through a pair of second- or even third-hand binoculars we quickly became expert plane-spotters. A couple of us even had cameras with which to record events that have become part of Canada's fascinating aviation history.

Take, for instance, that Sunday early in May of 1954 when Trans Canada Air Lines (TCA), renamed Air Canada eleven years later, put their brand new Lockheed Super Constellation on display. And what a plane it was! It was huge! It had four huge engines. The interior was huge. The triple-tail assembly was huge, too. Oh, did I tell you it was huge?

With two hundred- and three-hundred-seat planes pretty much the norm today, the *Connie* (that's what we experts called her) was pretty much of a small fry, having room for only sixty-three passengers and a crew of seven. But for us kids the chance to not only see but to actually be invited to walk through this, the newest addition to TCA's aging fleet of DC-3s and North Stars, was just as exciting – no, I think it was more exciting than witnessing the comings and goings of the Airbuses and 757s of today.

TCA had actually ordered the spectacular new plane in 1951, just four years after it first flew in commercial service, but because of development problems with the Curtiss-Wright radial compound engines (there's a power plant description you don't hear about any more) the delivery schedule had been seriously delayed. Potential TCA customers on the Montreal–London route were crossing the Atlantic in BOAC (now British Airways) Stratocruisers instead.

What got me to reminiscing about my youthful wanderings out into the hinterland around Malton ... oops, Pearson was a recent conversation I had with Philip Yull, a local businessman who has plans to rescue one of the few remaining Super Constellations in existence, transport it to Mississauga, and convert the craft into a conference centre/flight museum complex. The plane being considered for 'rebirth' is, interestingly, a former TCA Super Constellation, CF-TGE. This aircraft flew as part of the Maple Leaf fleet from 1954 until 1962 when it was acquired by World Wide Airways ending its career as one of Nordair's unserviceable aircraft at Montreal's Dorval Airport.

After several unsuccessful attempts to breathe new life into the now historic craft (of the 900 built by Lockheed only twenty survive), Philip has come up with a plan that has met with enthusiastic support from both the general public and many of the elected Mississauga city officials.

The inaugural flight of the Super Constellation, at Toronto's new airport, May 14, 1954.

Philip has asked that if any *Sun* readers would like to learn more about his plans or can contribute in any way to help rescue *Connie*, they are invited to give him a call at (416) 860-3214 or send him a fax at (905) 824-7646.

• • •

An eight-page newspaper describing John Hood's fascinating two hundred years of Toronto history mural on the Front Street East wall of the Toronto Sun Building is now available, free of charge, at the *Sun*'s reception desk at 333 King Street East (between Sherbourne and Parliament streets).

An interesting new board game has recently been created by Subway Games International. Called Subway Toronto, it's described as a game about getting around underground and is available in select game stores, for example, Dufferin Games, Brain Buster, and Mindgames. For further information call (905) 934-0539.

One last thing, to the lady who approached me in the Coles store in the Don Mills shopping mall (and whose name and phone number I didn't get), the old Hygeia Hall was at 40 Elm Street in downtown Toronto.

HAPPY 100TH, HIAWATHA!
July 2, 1995

A couple of weeks ago I wrote about the restored Toronto Island ferry *Trillium* which recently celebrated its eighty-fifth anniversary and during that period of time has safely transported hundreds of thousands of fun seekers to and from the Island or on special cruises around Toronto Harbour. Well, as old as *Trillium* may be there's another vessel that traverses Toronto Bay that's even older. In fact, on Sunday next, July 9, the Royal Canadian Yacht Club's sleek passenger tender *Hiawatha* will have been in service for precisely 100 years.

July 9 a century ago was a nice warm Tuesday, and at four o'clock that afternoon a large crowd had gathered at the busy Bertram shipyard on the water's edge near the foot of Bathurst Street. They were there to witness the launch of the Royal Canadian Yacht Club's (RCYC) new steel passenger tender that would replace the old clipper-bowed steam yacht *Esperanza* that had been doing yeoman service since 1881.

Prior to that date water transportation hadn't been a problem for RCYC members since the club was located (and had been since its formation in 1852) on the mainland side of the bay. But when the city announced major changes were in store for the central waterfront area, RCYC officials decided that the time was right to move across the bay to a quieter location on Toronto Island.

While the trusty *Esperanza* was perfect at the start, she soon became too small and the club was faced with the task of finding something more appropriate. But it soon became apparent that a new launch, especially one befitting the RCYC, would be expensive. Undaunted, they offered life memberships for sale and soon the necessary $7,000 (the going price in 1895 for a Bertram-designed and -built, sixty-five-foot steel passenger launch complete with boiler and compound steam engine) was raised. The order was placed with Bertram's on February 23 and in less than five months the vessel was ready to make her eagerly anticipated debut.

Taking part in the launching ceremonies were George Bertram, owner of the shipyard, and A.R. Boswell, the yacht club's commodore, who in addition to being one of the city's best-known lawyers had served as the mayor of Toronto in 1883 and again in 1884. Boswell still holds the distinction of

July 9, 1895. Workers at Toronto's Bertram shipyard ready the RCYC's new launch *Hiawatha* for the 4:00 pm launching. And there's not a hard hat in sight!

146

winning the mayor's position by the narrowest margin in the city's history with just five votes separating him from runner-up John J. Withrow.

Also present in the official party was Arendt Angstrom, the designer of the new vessel and a man who, a decade later, would create another long-cherished member of Toronto's waterfront flotilla, the proud lake steamer SS *Cayuga*.

One of the city's daily newspapers reported on the launching in these words:

> Mrs. Boswell broke the customary bottle of wine over the vessel's bow as she began to move on the ways [the ship not the commodore's wife - M.F.], and gave her the name *Hiawatha*. Down the hundred feet o ways the vessel slid and dropped from them into the water with perfect ease. The launch was decorated with flags and bunting, the burgee of the club flying from the bow and the blue ensign with the crown in the fly being carried on the stern.

While there is no documented proof as to why the name *Hiawatha* was selected for the new vessel, we do know that Indian names were very much in vogue with many thoroughfares on Toronto Island bearing Indian names; Manitou, Cayuga, Ojibway and so on. In fact, the name Toronto itself is probably derived from the language of the native people. In addition, Henry Wadsworth Longfellow's epic poem *The Song of Hiawatha* written forty years earlier was still enjoying great popularity. Interestingly, when the RCYC purchased another new boat nearly two decades later, it was named in honour of Kwasind who was described in Longfellow's poem as Hiawatha's "great, strong friend."

Over the years time and traffic combined to overtake *Hiawatha* and in 1982–83 the club decided to treat their trusted friend to a major rebuild. *Hiawatha*, complete with a modern diesel power plant, but looking every bit like it did when Mrs. Boswell broke that bottle of wine over the bow, returned to service on Toronto Bay on May 19, 1983.

Happy 100th *Hiawatha*!

Thanks to Harold Shield for material used in this column.

BIG BOATS ONCE COMMON
July 9, 1995

Today, the presence of a large ship of any kind in Toronto Harbour is a somewhat unusual occurrence. To be sure 'sugar boats' still call at the Redpath dock and lakers loaded with cement keep supplies topped-up at the batching plants located in the Terminal District at the east end of the harbour. But, for a variety of reasons (containerization, pipelines, to name just two) today's arrivals pale in comparison with the variety and number of vessels calling at the Port of Toronto even as recently as a couple of decades ago.

Absent altogether are the passenger boats that in the early part of this century seemed to fill just about every available slip along the smokey water-front as they either loaded local picnic groups or dis-

Passenger lake boat *Tionesta* puts down quite a plume of black smoke as it arrives in Toronto from its home port of Buffalo, New York, on June 16, 1931. Note a portion of the Terminal Warehouse building, now Queen's Quay Terminal, on the left.

gorged hundreds of visitors eager to visit the 'Queen City's' principal attractions, the main stores of Eaton's and Simpson's, the incomparable Ex, or "Sir Henry's folly on the hill," Casa Loma. In fact, back then Toronto's navy, consisting of such popular passenger lake boats as *Cayuga, Chippewa, Kingston, Toronto, Turbinia, Dalhousie City,* and a host of others including a flotilla of smaller Island ferries would do credit to many small nations.

One of the most interesting visitors to the harbour in recent years was HMCS *Toronto*, one of the Canadian navy's new frigates. I understand that on a recent tour of European ports the sleek craft did herself proud and was a splendid ambassador for both our city and country.

HMCS *Toronto* was by no means the first warship to sail into Toronto

Harbour. There have been submarines (both German and American) and, in 1959, a tremendous assortment of fighting ships from various NATO countries. But not all such visits have been of the friendly variety.

In fact, in April of 1813 a fleet of more than a dozen warships was spotted south of the Scarborough Bluffs and it was a pretty good bet that these 'visitors' weren't here on a goodwill mission. After all we were right in the middle of the War of

The mace arrived on board USS *Wilmington* shown here at anchor in Toronto Harbour, July 3, 1934. The Royal York Hotel and Bank of Commerce appear on the skyline while the passenger steamer SS *Kingston* gets under way to the left.

1812, or as many called it President Madison's War. In truth the ships were part of an American invasion force and their arrival was the precursor to a savage bloody battle and a lengthy occupation of our community during which several buildings were burned and various items of personal property stolen. Of particular importance was the capture of the mace, an artifact symbolic of legislative authority in the Province of Upper Canada (Ontario). More than 120 years later, and as part of Toronto's 100th anniversary celebrations, the mace was returned as a goodwill gesture initiated by President Roosevelt. It arrived on board another United States Navy vessel, the USS *Wilmington*, a 1,400-ton former gunboat that had fought in the Spanish-American War, but now as a training ship was void of any armaments.

It was during the *Wilmington*'s visit in early July 1934 that Fort York was rededicated. The fort's restoration was deemed to be a fitting tribute to the city which was celebrating its 100th year of incorporation in 1934. Not coincidentally, the labour-intensive project was just one of the many 'make-work' ventures carried out by various levels of government during the years of the Great Depression.

IS IT SIGNPOST TO RAIL TRAGEDY?
July 16, 1995

I'm still eagerly searching out material for a book on the origins of Metro street names. So far I've been able to trace several hundred of the several thousand throughout and while that number may seem small one has to remember that many

Overend Street, signpost of a tragedy or just another street name?

street names were selected by persons unknown simply because they sounded nice (Brassbell Millway, Alfresco Lawn), are descriptive of the location of the street (Lake Promenade, Woodland Heights), or, and boy these are the tough ones, were the names of family members: June, Rosalie, and Yvonne avenues ... were they all relatives of Jethro Crang, namesake of nearby Jethro Road?

But I shouldn't complain because if they were all easy – Simcoe, Yonge, etc. – the research wouldn't be any fun.

Take, for instance, the name of a small street (it's only a block long) that connects Front and Mill streets just west of the Don River. I drive past Overend Street on my way home from the *Sun* after dropping off my column (haven't got a modem yet nor do I want one – it's more fun meeting the people at the paper) and I simply surmised that it got its name simply because it's over at the end of Front Street.

However, one day while leading a tour through little St. Michael's Cemetery tucked away near the busy Yonge/St. Clair intersection I suddenly came upon a polished granite memorial to the late Harry Overend with the rather cryptic inscription "Greater Love Than This No Man Hath Than to Lay Down His Life for His Friend" and the date he was, as the description went on, "Accidentally Killed."

Calling up the March 23, 1916 edition of *The Evening Telegram* on the microfilm reader in the *Sun* library, I was suddenly transported back to the final day in the life of Harry Overend and perhaps given a clue as to why the little street was so named.

Fifty-seven-year-old Harry Overend was a highly experienced engineer

Sketch of the wreck site that appeared in *The Evening Telegram* **on March 23, 1916.**

with the Grand Trunk Railway. In fact, it was Harry who, whenever royalty or other special dignitaries were being transported by the GTR, would be assigned as that particular train's engineer.

On the evening of March 23, seventy-nine years ago, Harry was in the cab of the Chicago Flyer, a six-car, Toronto-bound Grand Trunk passenger train. At approximately 10:15 PM, just as the Flyer traveling at 60 MPH was approaching the small Port Credit station, its powerful searchlight beam picked up the murky outline of a small freight engine and tender straddling the track several hundred yards ahead. "Jump," screamed engineer Overend to his fireman Edward Heenahan and in less than a second Harry was alone in his cab. Heenahan rolled down the embankment to safety just as the still night air was slashed by an ear-splitting, metallic-grinding noise as the heavy locomotive struck the smaller engine.

Harry Overend's engine was derailed, ripped into a trackside ditch, and fell on its side where it was hit again and again by the trailing passenger coaches. In the bedlam and chaos poor Harry was decapitated.

And in the smaller engine, crushed into an unrecognizable mass of steel by the monster stream engine, both the fireman and brakemen also lay dead.

An investigation determined that the freight crew had erred in attempting to exit the siding following the passage of number 108, the Buffalo–Toronto train, instead of waiting for number 16 to clear as the official train order had directed.

Now, here's the quandary I'm in. Was the little street that decades ago pierced the busy railway yards that used to sprawl alongside the west bank of the Don River named by a grieving city in honour of Harry Overend, the late lamented hero of the Port Credit railway tragedy, or was it simply over near the end of Front Street? I wonder.

• • •

A reader sent along a photograph that she had found while cleaning out an attic. She assumes that it is a view of one of the many houses built by her father earlier this century here in Toronto and wonders whether any reader recognizes the building and can supply her with an address. Looks like a Rosedale residence to me. Anyone else have any thoughts? If so drop me a line and I'll pass on the details.

Recognize this house?

There were a number of responses to my request for the identity of the house shown in this column. As a result of these calls and letters, the trail has led to Burlington, Hull, Etobicoke, North York, or Toronto. Obviously, I'm still searching.

VINTAGE PLANES TOUCH THE SKY
July 23, 1995

A few weeks ago I received a letter from James Lloyd who operates Aviation Videos Ltd. in Burlington, Ontario. He suggested that with all the emphasis being placed on V-E and the upcoming V-J Day fiftieth anniversary activities and tributes, some *Sun* readers might be interested in a new VHS video he recently began stocking. *Knights with Wings* tells the story of the British Commonwealth Air Training Plan, a project that history would eventually describe as one of the greatest contributions made by any Allied country in ensuring a successful conclusion to the Second World War.

Boarding the versatile North Star at Malton Airport, circa 1950.

Courtesy *Toronto Sun, Toronto Telegram* Collection.

Originally shot in 1941 on 16 mm colour film by Gordon MacCormack (who first soloed in 1933 and went on to become one of the hundreds of flight instructors serving Canada during the war), this movie-turned-video documents the fascinating story of a young aviator-to-be's life at a typical RCAF Elementary Flight Training School. Of particular interest to any aviation buff are the colour sequences of the classic Anson, Norseman, Lysander, and Harvard aircraft once so prevalent throughout Canada and now only seen in museums, air shows, or in aviation history videos such as this.

Other elements of flight training including the use of Morse code, parachute packing, and instrument training using the ubiquitous Link trainer are also featured.

More information about this and other historical aviation videos (some feature the Toronto-built Lancaster, Mosquito, Arrow, and CF-100) is available from Aviation Videos Ltd., 2214 Courtland Drive, Burlington, Ontario L7R 1S4.

Incidentally, Gordon MacCormack, now an eighty-year-young retired insurance executive living in Maitland, Ontario, is donating the proceeds from the sale of this video to a local school whose video arts students helped him produce the tape.

While on the subject of airplanes, Larry Milberry, without question Canada's most prolific writer of aviation books having authored or co-authored at least a dozen, has another to his credit and this one is a dandy. Titled *Canadair: The First 50 Years* (which Larry co-authored with another aviation historian Ron Pickler) is an impressive 392-page hardcover book dealing with a Canadian company that started in 1911 as a small shipbuilding enterprise on the banks of the St. Lawrence River in the heart of Montreal. In 1944 Canadian Vickers Limited became Canadair and over the ensuing years the various aircraft that rolled off the company's busy production lines were familiar objects in the skies over our city.

Perhaps the plodding, but reliable, North Star was the most frequent Canadair visitor to Toronto. It was the workhorse of the Trans Canada Air Lines (Air Canada since 1965) fleet from the day it flew into old Malton Airport in the spring of 1946 until the last of its type was retired from the TCA roster in July of 1961 as the newer Vanguard turbo-props and revolutionary jet-powered Douglas DC-8s took over. Nevertheless, a few recycled North Stars could frequently be seen on the Malton tarmac, now in the colours of smaller airlines, for years after.

The book also describes a host of other Canadair products that were familiar to Torontonians, especially those who took in the annual air show at the CNE; planes such as the T-33 (a direct descendent of the United

States Air Force's first operational jetfighter, the F-80 Shooting Star), the remarkable Sabre, the CL-41 Tudor (the choice of the Snowbirds), the CF-104 Starfighter, CF-5 Freedom Fighter, the Yukon, Argus, and many others. Of special interest is the chapter on the unique CL-215 waterbomber so much in the news these days as raging forest fires continue to devastate hundreds of acres of Canadian timber. This aircraft is the only plane in the world to be designed specifically to fight forest fires. The first CL-215 took to the air in 1967.

An interesting sidelight describes the process by which the Spanish government purchased eight CL-215s. They were paid for with money obtained through the sale of that country's wine in the Province of Quebec. Spain did alright by the deal because Quebecers have developed a taste for the imported product and continue to buy it in great quantities, even though the water bombers have been long paid for.

The book also has a lengthy chapter on the Challenger business jet. There's another surprising Canadair connection with our city. The company was the prime development contractor for the Intermediate Capacity Transit Vehicles operating on the Scarborough RT (rapid transit) line.

Canadair: The First 50 Years is available (as are Larry's other books) from select bookstores or from CANAV Books. Call (416) 698-7559 for details.

THE CHANGING TORONTO SKYLINE
July 30, 1995

O f all the columns I've written in the *Sunday Sun* over the past twenty years (has it really been that long?), the type of column that results in the most reader feedback is the kind that features photographs of the same scene taken many years apart; like the views accompanying this column, for instance.

In both instances, the photographer pointed the camera up Bay Street from a point near that street's intersection with Queen's Quay. In the earlier view, taken in the fall of 1928, Toronto's skyline was dominated by just one building, the Royal York Hotel, which was just starting to take on the shape that we all now recognize.

The Royal York Hotel was built on the site of the Queen's Hotel, which for many years was the city's most popular hostelry and had on various occasions been the Toronto address for visiting royalty and a multitude of other well-heeled world travelers.

Although work began on erecting what would frequently be described with considerable pride in the local newspapers as Canada's largest building (as soon as the last fragments of the old hotel had been hauled away), the massive new structure wouldn't be ready to welcome its first paying guest, a Mrs. Kenneth Mackenzie visiting from Winnipeg (I guess back then married women weren't allowed to have their own first names), for two more years.

To be absolutely and totally *historically* accurate, the very first guest to sign the register of the new $16 million, 1,100-room hotel was the governor-general of the day, Viscount Willingdon, who, unlike Mrs. Mackenzie, didn't have to pay.

To the left of the Royal York in the 1928 photo is the Toronto Harbour Commission Building. When this handsome structure was ready for occupancy in 1918 the waters of Toronto Bay lapped at its front steps. In the intervening years landfilling has resulted in the building now being well inland. In fact, in the 1995 view it's hidden behind WaterPark Place, which itself was built on man-made land.

Emerging to the right of the hotel is the new Bank of Commerce Building on King Street which, when completed in 1931, was the tallest

Bay Street, looking north from
Queen's Quay, 1928

building, not just in Toronto or
even Canada, but in all of the
British Empire. Also seen in the
1928 photo is Peter Witt number
2732 southbound on the *Bay*
streetcar route. The line operated
between a loop at Queen's Quay

Same view, 1995.

and York Street to a loop just west of the St. Clair/Caledonia intersection via
Queen's Quay, Bay (in 1928 a temporary bridge carried the streetcar tracks
over the railway tracks), Bloor, Avenue Road, and St. Clair. In 1930 the new
underpass between Fleet (Lake Shore Boulevard) and Front streets precluded the need for the bridge and in the following year Davenport Road was
opened between Bay and Avenue Road and the Bay cars were then taken off
Bloor Street and rerouted via Davenport. With the opening of the Yonge
subway in 1954, the Bay line was abandoned. In an interesting twist, while
the surface streetcars may be gone, there are still streetcars under this part of
Bay Street operating on the Harbourfront line.

In the 1995 view the stately Royal York Hotel can still be seen, and
though it's not visible from this vantage point the Bank of Commerce is still
there, too. Other sky scratchers are the black towers of the TD Centre, the
gold (real gold, 2,500 ounces of it) Royal Bank Plaza, and the white Canada
Trust Tower. And slicing through it all the elevated Gardiner Expressway.